A ROUND WITH GOD

Matt Parsons

First Edition 2009

Copyright © 2009 Matthew J Parsons   ISBN: 978-184426-739-2

All Scripture quotations are taken from the New Living Translation © 2004 Tyndale. Used by permission.

Editing by Joe Clark and Steve Parsons

TABLE of CONTENTS

Forward

Introduction

Chapter 1: Not a Good Start

Chapter 2: Oh No - The Wheels Came Off!

Chapter 3: I Knew You Would Come

Chapter 4: A New Club in the Bag

Chapter 5: Bending the Rules

Chapter 6: You Are Disqualified

Chapter 7: A Game for All

Chapter 8: Never Too Late

Chapter 9: New Ownership

Chapter 10: The Last Round

Appendix

Foreword

Having been a Christian since 2002 and a PGA Golf Professional for 20 years; my first thoughts of a golf club, in Cornwall or anywhere else for that matter, seemed a strange setting for writing a book about Jesus Christ.

However, this wonderfully powerful account of the Gospel delivers a unique and simple understanding of the love of God and the need for all to experience Salvation through Jesus Christ. Matt's obvious sensitivity and personal walk with Christ will encourage all who love God and want to share His love with those they spend time with. This is true marketplace evangelism. Matt illustrates with compassion and love for his friends at the golf club how, when God's timing is right, we can bring God's message of hope to those in need.

This book is written around Matt's experiences of the game of golf, but the principles can be applied at any work-place or social venue.

If every sports venue had a 'Matt' spreading the good news of Christ's love then the world of sport would be in good hands.

May God bless all who read this book! Thanks Matt.

Andy Gorman,

PGA Golf Professional.

Introduction

The cliff path was well-worn, not by design, but established by thousands of others who had walked this way previously over many years. Overhead, a few seagulls glided aimlessly in a light breeze that gently touched my face as I slowly walked that same path, contemplating the words of Brian, a club golfer, as he was ready to tee off that morning. Brian was a rather large or should I say – extra-large guy who weighed in at over twenty stone, and yet in spite of his size, played a good game of golf.

I didn't know him that well, although he fitted well into his club nickname of 'Grumpy.' Brian often looked as though the world owed him a great debt, often complaining about everything and everyone and to find him smiling was as rare as a achieving a hole-in-one. I hadn't seen Brian around for a few weeks so it was good to see him one morning standing on the first tee. As he was about to tee off, I caught up with him. "Hi Brian, haven't seen you around for a few weeks." He turned, although he was about to tee off, and simply said "Oh it was my nephew. He just died and he was only three, so what's that all about?" Brian and his partners soon commenced their round of golf; I didn't play that day as I knew I needed some space to be still and contemplate.

By now I had reached the end of the path, and as I sat near the cliff edge, looking over the beauty of a glorious coastline of deep blue seas and golden sand, I began to reflect on Brian's question, "What's that all about?"

In my heart, I knew I longed for the opportunity to explain some of the basic truths I discovered in my own personal walk with God. I was convinced that somehow I needed to address not only Brian's question, but to address, above everything else, the very simple
message of the Gospel, the good news of Jesus Christ, and the transformation He brings to any individual who is prepared to stop and listen for a while.

As I waited for further inspiration, I clearly saw a wonderful link between my experiences at the golf course and my desire to share the greatest message on earth. That morning, a seed was sown in my heart to write this very down-to-earth but sincere little book, simply called 'A Round with God.'

I make no apology that the gospel message is included in most of the chapters as the book is not to be read as a novel, but as a personal testimony of actual experiences and each chapter stands alone. I have simply drawn parallels to the Christian message.

Although I have used first names, no surnames are included and for the personal stories of Brian, Tom, Keith and Bill I have sought and gained their permission.

Chapter One

NOT A GOOD START

Cyril, my brother- in –law, had been a member of Merlin Golf Club for a few months, prior to this my first visit. Although I had played a few rounds at Porthpean Golf Club with some friends, I did not regard myself as a golfer by any stretch of the imagination. Within a few weeks of playing my first round, I decided to join a golf club and welcomed Cyril's invitation to play Merlin with the view of becoming a member.

"So what's the course like?" I asked, as we drove down a steep hill leading to Mawgan Porth. Mawgan Porth is one of my favourite spots on the North Cornwall Coast and with its golden sand and high cliffs on both sides, it is a popular holiday destination. "It's ok, it's only a nine hole course at the moment, but I understand the owner has plans to extend it to a full eighteen hole course in the future" Cyril replied.

Looking back, I was more than happy to play nine holes as I was still having immense difficulty trying to understand why I ever started playing golf. To start with, I had no idea how or why I needed so many golf clubs, but it gave the impression, especially if I wore a Ping golf shirt, that I knew what I was doing. Reading and trying to understand the rules and the etiquette was another challenge. Then, learning the difference between stroke-play and match-play and all the various names and types of competitions almost brought on a nervous breakdown. That was before I was faced with the simple task of hitting a little white ball which had, and still has, a mind of its own.

We soon arrived at the temporary clubhouse, which was no more than a converted portable cabin. Not quite St Andrews, I thought, but thankfully neither were the green fees!
A few yards away I could see the ongoing construction of what was to be a new clubhouse.
My first impression however wasn't that positive. There were scattered pieces of discarded and rusted machinery and construction equipment all over and it looked as though a bomb had hit it. I needed Cyril to remind me that this was not the finished article and with that I began to look forward to playing some golf.

"Gentlemen, how can I help you?" were the first words I heard as I looked around the somewhat cramped conditions inside the cabin. Suddenly I saw Peter, who worked for the owners of the club. He was standing behind a makeshift wooden type counter, which acted as the natural barrier between employee and customer. Peter was about 5ft 7in tall, he had a fixed but unforced smile, a wicked twinkle in his eye and one of the most important characteristics anyone working with the public could offer; that important commodity called 'the ability to communicate and make a stranger feel welcome', which he did well.

"Hello Cyril", said Peter, "Who's this then?" taking a quick glance in my direction. "Matthew," Cyril replied. "Good to meet you Matt, now how can I help you?" Peter asked again.

Within a few minutes we had paid our green fees, picked up a scorecard, changed our shoes and were ready to tee off. That was the first of many rounds of golf as I decided to make Merlin my home course and become a member.

Over the next few years of my membership at Merlin, I realised and appreciated that Peter was always ready to share a tale or two from his vast knowledge and experience. He was a real asset to the club. Although he wasn't a golfer, he was a real sounding board to the many members and visitors who always looked for an opportunity to share; hole-by-hole and shot-by-shot in detail, the joys and disappointments of the round just played. When Peter left the club a few years later, we lost, in my opinion, one of the principle people responsible in helping create a unique atmosphere in the Merlin clubhouse. Although no longer involved with Merlin, Peter will never be forgotten by the members who knew him well. Thank you Peter. I hope you will have the opportunity to read these few pages.

Soon the new clubhouse was finished and it wasn't long before we were enjoying the benefit of our new surroundings. Over the next few months, the course was extended, new members joined and close friendships formed and, as though someone had hit the correct switch, even golf standards began to rise.

I have always enjoyed playing sport and although I played both football and cricket at a reasonable level, I was what one would call a good average club player. However one thing I did learn from an early age was that being a good or average sportsman was one thing, but being a sportsman who went to church and had a preaching ministry was altogether different.

I was told on more than one occasion, without saying a word about my faith, that while I was welcome to be a part of the club football team or cricket team, it would be wise to keep my 'religion' to myself. I had the usual chat from the senior member of the various teams I played for, about people not wanting religion jammed down their throats or not wanting any Bible-bashers around the changing room, usually with an after-thought which would add "Of course I don't mind personally, it's the other players who may get upset". I didn't mind the anticipated advice but often felt it was unjustified.

On joining Merlin, my attitude was the same as ever. I decided to leave my sandwich board at home, if ever I had one, and keep my preaching ministry stored away in the golf locker with a willingness to share my faith openly if and when there was an opportunity. Well, that was my intention, and all was going well but it wasn't too long before every member knew they had a preacher as a potential playing partner, and suddenly the atmosphere changed.

It was a Saturday afternoon and Cyril and I felt we had progressed enough and were playing at a good enough standard to enter one or two club competitions. Competitive golf is a totally separate game to just turning up and hitting a few golf balls around a park. This is when it suddenly becomes real and the bigger the occasion, the greater the challenge. To digress for a moment, I remember the first time I was invited to play in a Pro-am by a very good friend called

Alan. I had only been playing for a little while and I didn't really know what a Pro-am was all about, but was about to learn.

As I drove into Launceston Golf Club, the car park was full of people and there was a real buzz about the place. I had no idea how big the event was until I looked up and read the master scoreboard. I was shocked to see my name on display for all to see with my two friends (both called Alan) and a young professional called Bradley Dredge. (Golfers reading this will go "WOW!" Non golfers will think, "WHO?" Bradley Dredge is now one of the top golfers in Europe). At that stage I didn't know if I should laugh or jump in the car and head back to the safety of Merlin. However, we soon met up with our professional who was a perfect gentleman. As our start time approached we made our way to the first tee where to my delight, (just kidding now) I met the official starter who, microphone in-hand, was ready to announce to all of Launceston Golf Club and most of North Cornwall so it seemed, who it was who was about to tee off.

Soon those dreaded words were announced "On the Tee; Matt Parsons from Merlin Golf Club!" By now my mouth was dry, my knees decided to do an involuntary dance, my heart was coming out through my chest and my hands were conducting my knees. My golf tee felt like the size of a pin head as I tried to place my ball on it, but my hands just would not stay still long enough. Finally I addressed the ball and out of total panic somehow managed to hit it off the tee all of fifty yards into the rough. Thanks to my playing partners, we managed to get into the prizes on that day, but I discovered that competitive golf is a different animal which few golfers are able to tame.

That experience was but a memory as Cyril and I sat in the clubhouse discussing the good, the bad and the absolute ugly of the monthly medal we had just played, when to our surprise, Ross the owner of the club joined us. "Ok lads, good round?" he asked. I viewed the question with much suspicion as it was only a few days previously I achieved a golfing first at Merlin with my approach shot to the final green. It was an awesome shot; somehow it stayed on the same flight path as it cleared the boundary hedge, flew over the neatly parked cars and smashed through the clubhouse kitchen window. Thankfully I was insured, but no matter how much insurance I had, it did not remove the embarrassment I felt as I walked into the clubhouse that afternoon. No reference was made to that moment as the three of us continued to chat for a while and then Ross, continuing the conversation, asked Cyril what he did for a living.

"I work for the council as a workshop supervisor", replied Cyril. Ross had a lot of experience regarding plant and machinery and it was through his design and construction that Merlin Golf Club was born. They talked for quite a while before Ross turned his attention to me, "So do you work with Cyril?" Oh, I thought. How do I answer that one? "No," I replied thinking that a quick answer may close the matter.

"So what do you do?" Ross continued. I didn't answer immediately as I was thinking to myself of the best terminology to use. Should I say "A minister", or "An evangelist", or what..." but before I could get any further Ross continued "Come on, is it a big secret?" So before another word was spoken I said "I'm a preacher." Ross asked again just to confirm his ears were not playing tricks, "Yes, I'm a preacher."

If Ross was the official starter at Launceston Golf Club, it appeared to me that he could not have announced my profession to the assembled in the clubhouse any louder that afternoon than I had experienced at my first Pro-am. "We have a preacher here chaps! Yes sir, a PREACHER!" The result was almost immediate as I noticed the guys, as though conducted by some invisible force; turn slightly away as to avoid eye contact. Ross moved away with a type of Mona Lisa smile as I turned to Cyril and suggested that it was time to leave. "Bye all - catch you soon," was my normal final greeting as I left the clubhouse, but on this occasion I left quietly.

That evening I needed some space to think through what had just happened that afternoon. Why was it that those two words, 'a preacher', created such a reaction? Why was it necessary to make my vocation a public announcement? Why didn't Ross say in a loud voice, "We have a workshop supervisor or a mechanic or a teacher in our midst"? Perhaps it was a type of warning to the other golfers, a type of 'watch out there's a preacher about' statement which resulted in everyone diving for cover. But why the reaction? I convinced myself for a brief moment that it may have been a happy surprise or even astonishment that a preacher could play golf - after all, we are meant to be a pathetic type of individual who needs a prop to get us through life.

No, I was convinced the problem was not the fact that I was a preacher or a preacher that played golf, but that I was immediately placed in the same category as those who were continually pushing their own brand of religion on door steps, street corners or at any other venue where they may find a listening ear willing or not. I convinced myself that the rebuff I felt was not personal, rather what was to be avoided in the eyes of most, was what I represented or I would be more accurate to say, what many thought I represented.

It wasn't long before it became general knowledge amongst the members that Matt was a preacher and although the next few weeks felt as though I was on the outside looking in, I continued to enjoy the game and built a general confidence in the understanding of the other members that I was not about to quote chapter and verse every time we walked out to play a round of golf. Slowly, bridges and friendships were built. More members felt comfortable to have this preacher around, and eventually I was able to close the divide constructed by fear and insecurity, and reconnect with the general membership. Soon, and I think from a position of increased security, the banter started as one or two found it safe to begin to pull my leg about my walk with God. I knew I was finally accepted when one member put his hand on my shoulder, gave it a squeeze and said "You know Matt for a preacher you're not such a bad guy."

Many assume I grew up in a very religious family, but in truth, bar being encouraged to go to Sunday School which seemed to have lasted the whole day, my parents were not church goers themselves. Looking back I can see that with six children under the age of seven, myself being number five and my twin sister number six, by sending us to Sunday school it had the benefit of giving us a basic religious upbringing, gave my parents the benefit of some quiet in the Parsons household for a few hours at least and it finally gave our Sunday school teachers and other adults the opportunity to practice one of the great Christian values of patience.

I was not the perfect child. I still remember being marched home by some church members for (in their eyes) trying to ruin the meeting. Although they would try and put the fear of God in me by warning me that God would be very angry at my behaviour, I was more concerned about the anger of my parents when they were told of the reason their little angel was sent home. Thankfully none of the teachers actually were brave enough to knock on my parent's door so I would walk in simply saying it was a very short meeting or giving some other viable reason why I was home early. Then we had the visit to our household by the police following some shoplifting. Nothing serious, just a few bits and pieces my friend G and I thought were going free from one of the stores. Thankfully we were caught immediately; I don't think I would have continued with such a career, even if we were not found out, for I felt in my heart a terrible guilt and a real sense that God was very angry.

My teacher on Sunday was also my headmaster from Monday to Friday. In those days the cane was used as a means of punishment and I felt the full weight of the stick often. By the age of twelve I had reached the church drop off stage in life. No more boring meetings, long sermons, old hymns and angry looks, freedom had arrived, or had it? In a strange way I knew something was missing. It wasn't the religious service I was pleased to escape from, as I never really found them that helpful.

I can now understand something of what I could not grasp at the age of twelve. What was missing was content or experience. It was like giving someone a glass and speaking about the wonderful drink it could contain, but the drink was never offered. So the glass or the structure was on display every week but you came in thirsty and left bored and still thirsty. Within a few weeks however I found my missing part.

I had heard about some 'different' church meetings that were taking place in another chapel. Some of my older brothers and sisters had attended and I thought I would go along, if only for a bit of a laugh. The atmosphere however was full of life and something or someone was touching my heart. It was as though I belonged; I was sitting in a chair that felt right for me even as a troublesome twelve year old kid. Two young preachers were talking about Jesus, His love, His forgiveness and His death on a cross for the sins of the whole world. This was the content; the missing part. It wasn't religion with its must and must not's. It wasn't the boring sermons or the long hymns. It wasn't just singing or hearing about what Jesus had done. No, the missing part was Jesus himself.

The meeting soon was over and as a room full of people stood to sing the last song, I, this kid at the age of twelve, left my seat and instead of walking out, I walked past all the adults, who were still singing, and as I arrived and stood at the front of that little chapel, I simply knelt down and asked Jesus into my heart and life. For a moment, I could hear no one singing as it felt as though I had touched another world. The very presence of God was real, and it was flowing over me like some invisible waterfall. I don't know how long I knelt in God's presence; I remember as I got up, many were also kneeling around me.

Soon the meeting was over and as I walked out into the night, I knew I had met Jesus. He was real and still in my heart and life. That night as I pulled up the sheets and blankets in my snug bed I said my first prayer, just one word – "thanks."

Seven years later I was sitting in church, yes the same one I attended as a child, listening to a very lifeless presentation. I looked around and realised I was sitting in a dead church. My thoughts began to drift to the people who lived within our ever-growing community. "It's you they need," I quietly prayed under my breath whilst I maintained a type of fixed look of attention toward the preacher when suddenly I had my second remarkable experience with God. As I uttered my complaint, I clearly heard a call on my life to preach.

At the age of nineteen I was a very insecure lad. I was shy and reserved and I sat as near to the back of the church as possible. The call to preach seemed to be so strong that I was convinced God was calling someone else to this all important task and I just overheard the conversation. "Me?" I thought, "A preacher? Never!" But with God all things are possible and through a remarkable set of circumstances, I soon found myself standing in a pulpit ready to take my first meeting.

It wasn't the greatest sermon ever preached and it lasted for about seven minutes. The meeting was over in about forty minutes and the congregation on the whole seemed to be delighted! I still think their delight was in the fact that they were heading home at least twenty minutes earlier than normal and not because of the sermon they had just heard.

That was just over forty years ago and to this day I continue to share this wonderful new life Jesus offers, although I must admit my preaching now lasts a little longer than seven minutes.

I have shared this part of my journey in the hope that you, the reader can understand that I did not fall off some angelic cloud, was not brought up in a strict Christian home and never attended Bible college, although the latter would have helped. I am just an ordinary guy who has spent his life sharing the story of Jesus. It's a message about one man who has changed and continues to change the eternal destiny of those who are willing to gladly receive Him.

In meeting new members at Merlin, especially those who never played the game before, and even mature players who have played the game for years, I am often surprised by how many have their own preconceived ideas regarding the rules of the game. Most new members are ok with a little word in their ear when they are breaking the rules. However it is possible that any offer of help can be met with outward hostility, especially if they have been doing it the wrong way for many years.

I remember once playing with a guy called Mike and I pulled him up for throwing his ball out from behind some trees on to the fairway. "What are you doing?" I asked. "Taking a free drop from behind this tree," he replied. Now normally young trees are staked to protect them and at such times you can move the ball to the nearest point of relief, thereby making sure you do not hit the tree with your backswing or follow through when playing your shot. Mike's tree was ten feet tall, totally established and no way were you allowed a free drop. Neither could you just throw it out on to the fairway.

"No Mike, you can't do that," I informed him, but he would have none of it. "I have always done that," he answered back in a very forceful manner. Now Mike was a big strong lad who could inflict some serious damage, so for my own personal safety I replied that we would check out the rules when we arrived back at the clubhouse. He was soon told that he had broken the rules and his card was invalid. His preconceived ideas not only made him hostile but it also caused his disqualification.

As a preacher I fully understand that many people have preconceived ideas regarding God, Jesus and Christianity. Some have preconceived ideas about heaven and hell and I can understand the hostility, like Mike felt on the golf course, when it appears as though suddenly a preacher has turned up to 'put everyone right'. For me, it's not like that at all. I have discovered over many years that most people's preconceived ideas are based on nothing more than belief systems passed on from generation to generation.

Most people have never heard what true Christianity is all about. They may have heard about Jesus, but few really understand the reason why He lived and especially why He was crucified on a cross. It would be a tragedy after playing the golf course of life, if anyone arrived in 'Heaven's Clubhouse' to discover that their preconceived ideas were all wrong and that they were disqualified. My one and only desire in preaching or sharing with others, is to give not my preconceived ideas, but what the Bible says about our lives and the reasons why we ought to closely examine the message of Jesus.

Chapter Two

OH NO – THE WHEELS CAME OFF!

A sudden lack of concentration on my part as I drove off from a road junction, caused the driver of an approaching car to swerve, very quickly I may add, to avoid an accident. I'm not sure if he was in my blind spot or not, but I was very appreciative of the excellent driving skill the other driver used in what was a very close call. I sat for a few seconds gathering my thoughts when I noticed that the other driver had stopped his car and was now marching toward me with a rather angry expression on his face. His fists were clenched and his arms were waving up and down in quite an aggressive manner while at the same time his language did not reveal the happiest guy in the world. (In certain situations men can multi-task). I am amazed how quickly the brain can come up with possible solutions to potential danger, and within a couple of seconds I had worked out all the options available to me.

I decided against driving off at speed for two very good reasons. To start with, he was that close to my car that if I had driven away I would have knocked him down, and two, if I had by some chance missed him, I realised we were travelling in the same direction and I didn't fancy a duel with two cars on the public highway which I just knew would have happened. A third option was to eyeball him as I stood 6ft 1in and weighed in at over 220 lb, but that was soon dismissed as being very foolish as I only had one serious fight in my life and that was at school inside a boxing ring and I lost.

I thought I could have congratulated him on his driving skills, a type of appeal to his ego as most drivers think they are the best in the world, but I thought perhaps that would have been taken in the wrong way and so I decided to go for option four.

Having allowed him thirty seconds to express the obligatory "You idiot, you could have killed me, you shouldn't be on the road" and a few other choice sentences, I simply smiled and said "I'm sorry, I didn't see you - please accept my apology." If I had pricked a hand held balloon with a red hot iron he couldn't have been more deflated. He stood silent for a few seconds before he spoke again, "That's ok mate, we all make mistakes." As I drove past him, I thought I would give him a little wave but I thought he may have misread my intentions.

I am very conscious that one of my character weaknesses is impatience and it can easily come to the surface when behind the wheel of a car. I had (please notice the past tense) some pet hates, especially toward those who would continually tailgate. Now, I ease off allowing them to pass or discipline myself to continue to drive in a sensible manner. I had one very narrow escape which showed me that being reactive, or getting angry at other car users was not really that sensible or wise - but I learnt the lesson the hard way.

I had been praying and thinking about the need to fine tune my driving habits at a church meeting but I didn't expect God to move so quickly. I attend Wadebridge Christian Centre and it was late and the roads were very quiet as I drove home that night. Speed was the last thing on my mind as I noticed the headlights of a car approach rather swiftly from behind. He caught me up very quickly and decided to sit on my boot. Convinced he wasn't going to move I accelerated - he did the same. I went a little faster and he did the same. Wrongly I thought I would burn this little irritation off as I continued to increase my speed. Sixty-seventy-eighty-ninety miles an hour and he stayed on my boot not looking to pass or drop back. I was just contemplating moving up to 100mph when I had the shock of my life. Suddenly, this boy racer turned on his blue lights and I realised that because of my own rage I had been trying to burn off a police car!

The next ten minutes were interesting. I had a go at him for driving too close to my boot (not a wise move), and he looked around and searched my car with a very powerful hand held torch as though he was convinced I was carrying some illegal substance or immigrant.
"OK, where have you been tonight?" he asked sternly. All I could think about was 'ninety in a sixty zone' and how this Policeman was going to throw the book at me as I answered his question in an octave higher than my normal tone of voice. "Me! I have been to a prayer meeting. I'm a church minister and work out from Wadebridge Christian Centre. I really thought that you were trying to force me off the road!" At the same time I was quietly praying to anyone in Heaven within earshot.

"MY WORD – LOOKS CAN DECEIVE!" he responded and following a very in depth lecture he told me to go home. He followed me for the next five miles, at a distance, until he passed me on the next duel carriageway. As he drove past, rightly or wrongly I gave him a little wave knowing in my heart that my earlier prayer had been answered.

I realised that it can only take a moment for the wheels to come off (I'm not talking literally) when you are behind the wheel of a car. Your journey may be without incident when suddenly all can go wrong and you become a victim of your own or someone's wrong choice. Road rage is not a pleasant experience for anyone and neither is golf rage. Oh yes it happens on a regular basis, everything goes well until the wheels come off and at that moment an individual's character is soon displayed.

When a golfer starts to talk to his golf ball, his golf club or others golfers in a frustrated tone it is a sure sign that the wheels are beginning to wobble. Some statements totally contradict logic, like "I hit a perfect shot and it's gone out of bounds" or "That was in the hole all the way until the last foot." Today I was playing with Derek who quite sincerely shouted after his ball with a wonderful question, "Where are you going?" Then we have the directional shout of "Go right or left or drop" - but my favourite shout or request I hear quite often and have used myself many times is, "Please come back!"

To the non golfer this habit of talking to the golf ball may seem very strange, however I have yet to top the talking habits of a golfer I played against in an open senior's competition. Thankfully, he was not from Merlin. He talked to his golf club prior to and after he made his shot. If the shot was good, he gave it a little pat on the head and said "well done." If the shot was poor, he would tell the club all about it. Following three or four bad drives with his driver, I saw him hold the club around its neck and he proceeded to dress this poor club down. I can't remember all the details but it sounded something like this; "I have just about had it with you! I don't think you are even trying today so you listen and listen well. One more bad shot from you and you're back in the bag and I won't let you out for the rest of the day!" He also used a lot of other words which I will not put into print! I had the impression that he needed a holiday or an appointment with an appropriate person. I kept my distance throughout the round as I wasn't sure of what may have happened if he missed a six inch putt or lost a ball.

This wonderful game can be so frustrating. Most players have spoken to their golf ball in flight from time to time and even the professionals are known to have a word or two. However golf rage is something else and over the years I have witnessed a few players at Merlin who have simply lost it and gone over the top when the wheels came off. I have seen clubs thrown down or thrown over the hedge in anger. I have seen putters bent and golf bags being kicked around like a rag doll. 'Chucker', when off the golf course was a pleasure to be around and I enjoyed his company, however when things went wrong, pure anger would get the better of him and soon the clubs would begin to fly in all directions. More than one golfer had cause to confront his behaviour on the golf course following his outburst of anger and frustration. He had a hair-trigger temperament and any wayward shot could easily set it off.

It was quite noticeable that I hadn't seen Chucker around for a few weeks when I asked a few members if anyone knew what happened to him. I was told that he had left as he was upset at being accused of chucking his clubs around. "Not half as upset as the guys he almost hit on occasions," I thought. I just hope I didn't influence his decision when following his return from a golf trip, which I think was overseas, I asked him how many clubs he returned with. Obviously I said it with tongue in cheek and I do hope he didn't take it too seriously.

A few words on one occasion caused the wheels to come off when I was playing the round of my life. I hadn't been playing for long but I had a natural swing (or at least a swing natural to me) and good hand eye coordination. During the round I was very pleased with the way I was playing. It was the monthly medal and my playing partner was marking my card as we stood on the sixteenth tee with three holes to play. "You could win this. You are ten shots under your handicap," said my partner. I suddenly developed an involuntary muscle reaction called tension. My brain was telling me to relax and keep playing golf but my emotions were shot. I just couldn't keep it together.

Those words "ten under handicap" somehow convinced me that the medal was mine. But as I prepared to drive, where as before I was totally relaxed and not thinking about hitting the ball, I now had many thoughts racing through my mind. "Ok, Matt relax, keep steady, don't try and hit it, It's only a game. What difference will it make if you win or not? Just keep playing as you have been. Don't grip the club so hard. Take a couple of deep breaths." A slow backswing was followed by an awful downswing and I just made enough contact with the ball to slice it into the rough. A couple more hack out's followed, then with a couple of more shots to the green. The hole was over.

The seventeenth and eighteenth holes were no better and I felt really disappointed when I found out that those three holes took twenty two more shots and the overall result revealed I had lost the medal competition by one shot. Sitting in the clubhouse the normal questions were asked, "How did you do Matt?" "Oh," I wanted to reply, "I was doing really well with only three to play then So-and-so opened his big mouth and told me I could win it because I had only dropped three shots and I went to pieces!" But remembering Who and what I represented I simply said "The wheels came off."

We all know this to be true. We are going well, life is rosy and we have no real issues that concern us, when suddenly in a moment the wheels come off. It may be a broken relationship, sudden sickness, financial crisis, loss of employment or one of many other reasons which can meet us on the path of life and change our direction and outlook regarding our future. Every experience in life can make us better or bitter. This may sound strange to the totally competitive golfer or to anyone who sees life through the eyes of success or failure, but as I look back to that day I am thankful that I failed to win the competition. It made me stop and take a long look in what I call my 'character mirror' and I wasn't impressed by what I saw. How easy it was to blame someone else for my inability to finish the game well. How quickly I found myself entering into some kind of blame culture, which incidentally is a major character fault in most of us. I fully appreciate that some who read the next few words may not agree with what is written, but I trust you will understand some of the following;

1) This world is not perfect in justice or righteousness.
2) If it was God's intention for man to live in harmony with Him and to be perfect in all his ways, then spiritually speaking, the wheels have come off.

It may interest you to know that the Bible has recorded clearly for us several chapters detailing how the wheels came off. Scholars call this 'The Origin of Sin.' It teaches us that when God first created our world it was good. Perfect in fact. But as a result of a great rebellion in heaven, Satan was cast out of heaven to the earth, and he set about destroying every good thing God had made. He convinced Adam and Eve that if they rebelled against God by eating from the Tree of Knowledge of Good and Evil, they would become wise and would know all truth. And although God had declared that the moment they took the fruit of that tree they would die, Eve was tempted to test God to see if it was true. She took the fruit and also gave it to Adam. Indeed their eyes were opened as they ate the fruit. The relationship with God was immediately broken as Adam and Eve, now aware of their sin nature, hid from God. Both physical death as well as spiritual death followed as man, like Satan before him, was separated from God.

The sin nature soon followed the first family and within one generation, Cain killed his brother Abel. The New Testament writers confirmed thousands of years later that "sin came into the world through one man" (Romans 5:12). Paul continued with "death came into the world through sin, so death spread to all men because all men sinned." Adam represented all of mankind in the Garden of Eden and his sin therefore affected the whole of mankind. The truth is, we only need to look at ourselves and world history to agree that it is true that we have all sinned and fallen short of God's standard. This isn't a surprise to us. The wheels have come off in our relationship with God.

Recently sitting at the golf club I overheard a conversation between two golfers who had just completed a round of golf. One player said "Oh the wheels came off, but thankfully I was able to put them back on again." I smiled as I thought of God's promise that He would make a way for His relationship with us to be restored to its former glory. God declared in the Garden of Eden that He would make a way for the total restoration of the whole of mankind.
He declared that He would personally come into the world and through sacrifice, suffering and death, would make a way for us to put the wheels back on again in our relationship to Him.

Sin is a terrible taskmaster. It takes you further than you want to go, keeps you longer than you want to stay and costs more than you want to pay. The problem is that sin comes so naturally to us. It runs in our veins. We are born with the desire to live life by our own rules. But sin ultimately leads to death, not just of the physical body but it closes the way into eternal life in heaven with God. Sin leads us all to hell, a place of death and darkness and an eternal destiny away from God.

This is because God declares himself to be completely righteous. Even though He is a God of great love and mercy he is also just and fair. Someone has to pay the price for our sin - but God has done something truly incredible. He sent His son to die and pay the penalty for our sins. That's why He declares that faith in Christ alone brings salvation to man. It is through faith in the fact that Christ was punished in our place on a cross that our relationship with God is able to be restored. Your personal relationship with God may be broken but Christ has made a way for personal restoration. This little book will show you how it is possible.

Chapter Three

I KNEW YOU WOULD COME

Ross was a little reserved and very much within himself as I walked into the clubhouse following another steep learning curve on the golf course. It was one of those times when wisdom was required as to when and when not to enter a conversation. The atmosphere did not require you to walk on egg shells; neither would you enter with a brass band playing. It just needed an awareness that all was not well. "Everything OK Ross?" I asked, half expecting a nod and short sharp reply, but was surprised by his answer; not so much for the content, but for the openness of his emotion as he spoke quietly yet with concern. "Mother isn't too good, no, in fact she's not well at all," he answered, with a slight quiver in his voice. Ross had a deep respect for his mum and although we never discussed his family or his family life as he grew up, I had come to know and appreciate that underneath the hard exterior Ross portrayed, there was a man with real emotion who would often show wonderful generosity.

On one occasion Cyril, my brother-in-law, and I had a conversation with Ross regarding a three man competition at Trevose G.C. We had never played the course and so we asked Ross, who had played the course on many occasions, for some information. I'm not sure if we were serious in our intent to enter the event, as we would have needed a third player, but as we were now getting around Merlin without causing any serious damage, we thought playing another course would be an interesting change. "Have you a third player?" Ross asked, and before we could answer he declared his intention to join us. "I will enter us as a team," said Ross and with a sly smile added that it was my job to look after the weather. Ross paid for everything but wasn't too impressed when we arrived at the clubhouse to find heavy rain and black skies. He mumbled something about not getting the weather right and asked if we (that's God and I) had fallen out. I assured him we hadn't and that I thought the weather would be fine. I'm not sure if it was a faith statement or not but five minutes before we were due to start our round the rain stopped and the sun began to break through the clouds.

"Would you like to tee off first?" I asked Ross as I began to place some sun block on my nose. By now he was struggling out of his wet suit as I looked up and said a quiet "thanks." We played our 18 holes in the dry and five minutes after leaving the course the skies opened and down came the rain. "That was lucky!" said Ross", "Perhaps" I replied.

Following our brief chat I decided to visit 'Mum' Oliver. "Peter, where does Mrs Oliver live?" "Next door" Pete replied. "Next door to whom?" I asked again. "To me" Pete replied. "Ok Pete, lets start again. Where do you live?" Soon I had the information I wanted and I began to find my way toward the small village of St Mawgan.

Set in a valley, very close to Newquay Airport is the picturesque village of St Mawgan. I was soon knocking on

Mrs Oliver's door. "Come in" she cried out, "the door is open."

I opened the door "Hello, hello, Mrs Oliver?" "Come in" once more she insisted. I was a little concerned at her open welcome. I knew my intentions were to encourage her in her sickness, but I was fearful that not all visitors would be so inclined. "Excuse me for not getting up, my legs are not what they used to be" she said with a slight frown on her face. I was not sure but I felt the frown was hiding a moment of pain. "I'm Matthew, Ross's friend. He told me you were not well so I thought I would pop in and say hello, if that's ok?"

"That will be lovely," she said. Her voice was soft and welcoming. I stayed for a while and I was privileged to learn just a little of Mrs Oliver's story. I explained that I was a minister within the church and that with her permission I would like to pray for her. A few minutes later, following a little more conversation and a prayer I left Mrs Oliver, carefully closing the door firmly behind me. No one knew of my visit, but Mum Oliver soon told Ross and a few days later he expressed his thanks for my visit.

Friendships are formed within any golf club and Merlin has always had a great reputation for friendliness and welcomes members and visitors alike. I well remember walking through the clubhouse one morning when Nick, the captain that year, was introducing a prospective couple for membership to the golf club. I'm not sure if he was having difficulty trying to get them to become members but as I walked by he informed them that Merlin even had its own vicar for any spiritual needs. I am thankful for the friendships formed with various members over the past 14 years. I have found it a joy and a privilege to be a part of so many lives, if even for a brief moment.

One very good friend was (and still is) Keith, who was in his early forties when we first met. He was a single guy, although he had previously been married, but was now living at home with his parents. Keith found in golf a welcome friend. The possibility of achieving the ambition of becoming a single handicap golfer gave him a goal and an aim which I think he lacked in his employment. Soon Keith was appointed Club Captain, an honour that ought to receive a measure of great respect. The captain is a leader and an ambassador for the club and the men he represents. He is an organiser, a diplomat, an administrative genius and it helps if he knows all the rules of golf. Keith worked extremely hard during his appointment and for the next twelve months it seemed as though he lived at the club, for such was his dedication.

As I said, friendships are important and I value them highly. We share our joys and when permitted, the sorrows we all can know so very well, as I was soon to discover. On one of my visits to the club I was told that Keith had lost his mum quite suddenly. Apparently she had collapsed one morning at home and died. I cancelled my round, found out (not from Peter) where Keith lived and began my journey to the family home.

As I drove those few miles I contemplated the visit I was about to make. Would I be welcome? Would Keith rather leave friendships on the golf course and keep private matters just what they are, private? Before I had the chance to answer such questions I was soon walking down the path to the door of the property. I knocked. Keith answered the door. He had a surprised look on his face as he saw me standing there, but I was soon invited in. Obviously the family were heartbroken over the death of such a loved family member. The kettle was soon boiling and over a hot cup of tea, I heard so much about Mum that I felt that I knew her. We talked about the family and found some special moments of joy and yes, even laughter. As I drove away I thought about the other friends at Merlin and some of the real issues they were facing both good and difficult.

In golf we often share our good shots; if you hang around the clubhouse after a round, you will always hear someone explaining how they achieved a birdie at the par 5 third, or a two on a par 3. Rarely do they tell you about the ball in the pond on the first or the eight or nine on the card. However, I have noticed that in the affairs of every day life, many of us act in the same way. We share our good shots. We often give the impression that we have it all together; that life is great without any problems whatsoever. We inwardly judge by the external values seen and noted in another; the new car, the location and size of the property, the bank balance and even the golf equipment used. And yet this somewhat appearance of value, actual or implied, does not always tie up with the truth of what's happening in our real world.

"The value of a man is not found" Jesus said, "in what he may own." Yet many live in this superficial life style, almost afraid to open up the deeper chambers of the heart and allow the bad shots of life, the wrong decisions, the guilt of past sin, the addictions known, the financial pressures to flow out and meet the love and wise counsel of God. "Don't talk to me about God!" someone once said to me; "I have enough problems already." Perhaps we convince ourselves that no one is interested and after all, we arrive at the golf club to play golf, not for some counselling session. Absolutely true; and may that always be the case. The issues of the heart and pressures of life should not be discussed when someone is about to hit a four foot putt. But what is hidden in the locker of life?

A few months had passed since the death of Keith's mum; little did we know that Keith would have been hit by another bad shot so soon. Having just finished a series of meetings in Wales that had lasted for nine days, I returned home to Cornwall, looking forward to my next round of golf. Soon I was walking into the clubhouse looking for a game. "Is everyone ok?" I asked as I walked into the bar. On the whole, yes it was, but I was soon to discover that it was not the case with Keith.

Just a few days previously, Keith was called off the golf course. His dad had collapsed and was rushed to hospital. "How is he?" I asked. I soon discovered that Keith had lost his dad. The clubs were not used that day and I was soon in my car travelling those same few miles to the family home. As I walked down the path to Keith's house, it reminded me of the same walk a few months previously. Who would have thought the same journey would be made again within such a short period of time?

Once more I knocked; the door opened and standing there was Keith. I will never forget the next five words he spoke. "I knew you would come." Soon the kettle was boiling and over a few cups of tea and coffee we sat and chatted for a while. Keith talked about the day he was called into hospital, the decision to turn off the life support and the wonderful memories he had about his dad. Soon, I was walking back down the path carrying something of the burden and empathy of Keith's heart.

In the times of life's 'bad shots' is God interested? Does He really care? Yes He does. The bad shot in golf (and we have all played them) is a direct result of one of the foundational truths being ignored. The stance may be incorrect or the swing plane of the club may be incorrect. The position of the grip on the club will certainly have a factor in addition to many other little bits that may be slightly out. The bad shots in life are a result of man's disregard for some foundational truths which were written many years ago. Consequently, no matter how hard we might try, we will never achieve 'the perfect round'. No matter how much we try to avoid it, trouble comes to us all. Whether that trouble comes as a result of our own choices, or whether we are hit out of nowhere (as in Keith's case) by the pain and suffering of our broken world.

I can give a very simple example here as I remind myself of my art lessons at school. Art was not my best subject; in fact I soon discovered I had paint by pass when it came to creative art. I enjoyed it to a degree, but no matter how hard I tried, I could not master the principles.

One day out of total frustration, my art teacher decided to move me from the Art class and introduce me to the potter's wheel. Wow! What excitement I felt as I threw the clay on the wheel and began to move the wood bar, neatly placed under the wheel, to and fro with great enthusiasm! I saw a picture of a wonderful vase in my mind's eye as I began to try and move the solid lump of clay into a beautiful upward shape. In reality however, the clay was all over the place and soon my teacher arrived, shouting as she came toward me in rather large strides, "You have got to centre the clay; you will never make anything unless the clay is centred on the wheel."

A life out of centre with God will have the same effect. We struggle to create anything of eternal value. We live according to our own selfish desires and the fruit of such choices is evident for all to see. We struggle with bad shots as we continually feed the old sinful nature and the results are found in our behaviour one toward another. As we saw in the last chapter, our first earthly parents, Adam and Eve, decided to rebel against God and life for them became out of balance. Since that time, we have evolved in all aspects of life; from education to science and from medicine to travel but in one fundamental area we have stayed still and that is in our character. In our first family we find anger, envy, jealousy and murder. Today those behaviour patterns are still found within our hearts as well as a whole list of others.

The truth is, we have all sinned and have played some bad shots; and we have all been affected by other bad shots that have come our way. So where is God at such a time? Where is He now in your pain and sorrow as you open the locker of your heart? The answer is simple; He is walking down your path.

In the last book of the Bible (called Revelation), are recorded some words of Jesus that He made to the church, but that have wider implications for this chapter. Jesus said "Look! I stand at the door and knock. If you hear my voice and open the door, I will come in, and we will share a meal together as friends."

Over the years I have encouraged many to open the door to Jesus and for those who have decided to take such an action, I have always known Him to be faithful to His promise.
When man makes contact with God, even in the most difficult of circumstances the possibility of a miracle can take place. I have had the joy of calling on the name of the Lord when praying with the sick, the broken, the depressed, the addicted and in many other situations. As I have opened the door of faith to Jesus I have never been disappointed. As I have seen His love and grace meet individuals, sometimes in the bad shots of life, I have inwardly given a word of thanks by simply saying, "I knew you would come."

Chapter Four

A NEW CLUB IN THE BAG

"This is the best club, without any doubt, I have ever bought. It's fantastic, magic, awesome!" said Brian as he showed me the shiny new club he had in his bag. Coming from Brian, who had purchased enough golf clubs over the years to open a small golf shop, it was quite a statement. Brian hits a good ball, and although his shape and size prevents a classic swing, he has the ability to play well. We had started the round well, the first two holes being played to par. I began to think that this was going to be a good day of golf as the conditions were perfect. The sun was warm, there was very little breeze and everything looked good. In the distance a couple of rabbits were dancing in the clover. Swifts were sweeping across the green fairways and it seemed like nature itself was enjoying the moment. Brian was now standing on the third tee and soon his ball was sailing through the air only to quickly land in the rough.

For the non-golfer, the rough is anywhere on the course where your ball has landed away from the nice short grass which runs from tee to green called the fairway. It's something to be avoided if at all possible. As we walked ever closer to our respective shots (modesty prevents me from saying where my shot landed), I noticed that Brian's ball was hardly visible as it lay in a patch of thick grass at the foot of a bank. It resembled a mushroom just breaking through the grass, sitting, waiting to be picked or hit according to how good your eye sight was.

Merlin, in addition to its excellent course which is improving year upon year, produces an excellent crop of mushrooms, if only for a few weeks in the year. I should add here that the growth is spasmodic and that the mushrooms are only found in small patches. During one seniors match, against a visiting team (name withheld to avoid embarrassment) I was amazed to see a fairly elderly gentlemen, whose eyes were not all they perhaps once were, address the top of a mushroom with the full intent of chipping it sixty yards on to the green, until his mistake was pointed out to him.

By now Brian had reached his ball. Taking out 'the best club he had ever bought' he took a couple of practice swings, convinced his new club would send the ball skyward, straight down the fairway and on to the green. Brian addressed the ball with a look of quiet confidence. I watched silently as, following a totally committed swing, the ball flew out of the jungle, hooked left and landed in the field next to the fairway, totally out of bounds. Looking down the fairway with great expectation he cried out, "Where did it go? Did you see it? Is it on the green?"

Oh, the look of unbelief when I pointed out, trying very hard to be serious, that his ball had flown over the hedge and landed in the field. "What! Never! Is that out of bounds then?" asked Brian in disbelief. I have noticed how golfers ask some great questions, especially when they cannot believe the obvious. I have seen balls disappear into a water hazard so hard that it has produced a splash like a diver jumping into a pool, balls sailing out of bounds and a number of equally punishable shots followed by the strangest questions. "Did it go out? Was that my ball? Does that one count?" Brian's club was returned to his golf bag in a manner that resembled a javelin thrower warming up. He mumbled something under his breath and took a big sigh.

Brian's triple chin was now resting on his chest as he took out another club, dropped another ball back on the original spot and chipped it further down the fairway.
I avoided saying anything for a few yards. I played my ball, turned to Brian and said, "So, what's that new club called?" By now Brian was laughing as he informed me that it was called a 'Rescue Club.' "But it didn't work, did it!" he chuckled. I have noticed, and have written previously, that some players have a personal love/hate relationship with their golf clubs. Often club golfers will arrive at the golf club with a new club in hand or even with a new set of clubs convinced that the recent purchase will make all the difference to their game. However like a good relationship gone wrong, the clubs can soon be out of favour. Separation soon follows and a new set takes the place of the old.

Swearing on the golf course happens on a regular basis, mostly when bad shots are played. Although I'm a committed Christian, I didn't fall off a cloud and I'm not that affected when guys let out a string of ablatives in a moment of frustration. In the club itself, the majority of members know that I'm simply a Christian who loves his God and enjoys his golf. I don't go around pushing my evangelistic message at every opportunity, but when asked about my relationship with God or what Christianity is all about I would be unfaithful if I kept silent. There have been a few times when I have been playing well that a question has been thrown into the mix for the sole purpose of trying to take my mind off the game. Some golfers will try anything!

Merlin has an in-house warning system for new members who may be playing with me for the first time. They are usually taken aside and simply told that they are playing with Matt, the preacher, so mind your language. I'm not sure if it is to protect the new member or me, but I appreciate the sensitivity of those who care enough, perhaps for both of us to avoid too much embarrassment. However some of the guys who would not be seen dead in a church building (except perhaps once - at the end of their life), and who naturally swear for a pastime, have shown a high level of restraint when I've played golf with or against them. These guys have no pretence, they are seen for what they are and I have a lot of time for them. I for one would never judge or try and change them by some religious code of conduct, which even the best among us would struggle to achieve. Jesus spent time with sinners, publicans and tax gatherers who would sell their own grandmother for a few extra quid. He sat with those who failed as well as with those who succeeded and is never surprised by any sin or attitude that we may discover in ourselves.

He loved being with humanity and loved teaching about the Kingdom of God. He loved showing fallen humanity an alternative, a hope for eternity and a love that even the hardest heart would find hard to resist. For my part, I always try to meet folk where they are, no matter what that means, and introduce them to the pure undiluted love that God has for them. I respect them and in my experience, most return the same.

One guy had slipped through the Merlin early warning net and we met up one morning on the first tee to play a competitive knock-out match. I can honestly say that I can't remember who he was though he is not a member now. He swore all the way around the first nine holes and it seemed that every other word contained four letters. I did ask him to keep his voice down and as there were ladies on the course, would he curb his language? He looked at me as though I had just come from Mars. "That's a joke, the !^%**! ladies are just as bad as the rest of us and some are worse!" "Not all" I replied and left it at that. He was a far better golfer than I was and after nine holes he was winning easily. As we stood on the tenth tee he turned to me in a somewhat aggressive manner and asked "So what's your job then?"

"Oh! I'm pleased you asked me that," I replied. "I'm a minister." "A minister of what?" he asked in quite an abrasive tone. "Oh sorry, I should have explained. I'm a church minister." I can honestly say I have never seen anyone go so white in just a few seconds. The blood drained from his face, he began to shake and he couldn't hit his ball from that moment with any conviction. By the sixteenth it was all over. He didn't say a word, not even well done. He stormed off, threw his clubs into his car and drove out. I simply shook my head in disbelief still thinking to myself, what was all that about?

"Brian" I asked, "So what's the thought behind a rescue club?" "I guess, to rescue you from a difficult place" Brian replied. Well I'm not sure if every golfer needs such a club in his or her bag, but I am convinced we all need rescuing from a very difficult place. One of the hardest tasks I have as a preacher is to try and open the eyes of the blind, the ears of the deaf and the lips of the mute. Of course I refer to the spiritual life of individuals and not the physical, although Jesus has and still continues to heal the sick. However, the spiritually blind refuse to see the truth, the spiritually deaf refuse to hear the truth and the spiritually mute refuse to talk about the truth. Some just get very angry, very defensive and storm off.

Please stay with me for a sentence or two as I explain what I mean by being rescued. God has declared that not one of us is perfect and that we have all fallen short of His standard. Many years ago I failed an examination by two marks; fifty percent was the pass and I achieved forty eight percent. "Are you going to fail me for the sake of two marks?" I asked my tutor. The reply was straight to the point. "Two marks or forty two marks short, it matters not. You still fail." The point was made.

I think if God would settle for 'reasonable behaviour' as a pass mark for Heaven most of us would take it off the tee, so to speak. The problem is God will not compromise, and the pass mark into Heaven is one hundred percent perfection. Which means we are all stuck, for none of us is perfect. We need rescuing. The pass mark into the Kingdom of God is not achieved by our good works or by our own self righteousness. You cannot go to Heaven by going to church, reading your Bible or even saying prayers. You cannot go by way of confession to a priest or by saying that you were christened as a baby.

Tom is one of our top golfers at Merlin. He is well respected as he serves the community as a police detective, undertaking a very important role. Within the next few months, Tom will be Club Captain and it will be a joy serving under his leadership. One day I was sitting at the bar in the clubhouse when suddenly Tom came over and spoke, almost in a whisper. "Something has happened to me. I don't want anyone to really know about it, but I have had a real experience of God". What Tom didn't know was that following a chat I had with him when he shared about his step-dad dying, I and a few others had been praying for him on a regular basis.

"So what happened?" I asked trying to give a quiet controlled answer, while inwardly I was jumping up and down rejoicing. "I was out on the road, when suddenly this lorry was coming up behind me, I lifted my hands and said "God I am yours," and something has happened, but can you keep it quiet?" We spoke for a few minutes about becoming a Christian, and we arranged to meet at his home the following week so that we could talk through what being a Christian was all about. Within a few days I was sitting with Tom and his lovely wife Hanna. I learnt more about horses in thirty minutes than I had learnt in fifty years owing to Hanna's expertise. Soon we were talking about what had happened to Tom. I explained that being a Christian was about having a restored relationship with God and not about trying to keep a list of do's and don'ts, must and must not's. We agreed that we had all sinned and I then shared one of my favourite verses in the Bible being "The wages of sin is death, but the FREE GIFT of God is eternal life through Jesus Christ."

"You know Tom", I continued "What this verse is saying is that God is offering us a free gift. Eternal life. All of our sins, past, present and future were laid on Jesus Christ so we could be forgiven. The cross, Tom, is where Jesus laid down His life and became God's eternal sacrifice for sin. It's the place where we meet the grace of God and accept by faith God's free gift of forgiveness and salvation."

That night, Tom accepted Jesus. As we prayed a very simple prayer I could sense that something very real was taking place in Tom's life. "Wow, that's amazing", said Tom when he finished his prayer. It was a wonderful evening. Of course I was to keep it all very quiet, but I was not surprised when out of this new found relationship with God, Tom got a Bible, started to pray and even came to church. In addition he started to tell others about this wonderful new life he had found in Jesus.

Yes, Jesus came to rescue all of us who have sinned and fall short of God's high standard. The question we must ask ourselves is a simple one; "What will I do with God's free gift of salvation?" Jesus has paid the price; all can be saved and all can be rescued from a lost eternity. The Rescue Club is designed to get you out of danger. Do you have one in your bag?

The rescue man – Jesus Christ, came to save you. Will you invite Him into your heart?

Chapter Five

BENDING THE RULES

I have missed John at Merlin over the past few months. An eye condition which has affected his ability to see correctly, has curbed his visits and stopped him playing the game he enjoyed immensely. Having the worst controlled slice I ever saw on a golf course, John was able to hit his ball from right to left (being a left handed player), way out of bounds, over fields and the rough and see it finally slice back into the fairway. To the non-golfer it could best be described as a very well curved banana shot. I had often thought that if John had hit a straight shot it would have surprised everyone playing with him but it would have added thirty yards to his drive.

Although not a great golfer, John played the game as it ought to be played. It was no great disaster for him if he took a six or seven or more. It wasn't the end of the world if he hit his ball into the water or even lost a ball or five during his round. For many reasons, John was a great man. I have met some men who are great golfers but have not yet learned, or have forgotten, that greatness in life is not determined by outward performance, position or personal possessions. Jesus once gave some sound advice when he said, "It is that which comes out of the heart which determines the quality of an individual." To see players throw their clubs in their car and drive out of the car park in a cloud of dust because they are upset over the way they played is not the best view in the world and it does nothing for that individual's reputation.

I have had some of my most enjoyable rounds of golf with some guys who would easily fall fowl of the trade description act, if golf was a product. Many times I have walked off the last green with those who have simply said how much they have enjoyed themselves, and the strange thing is they mean it in spite of playing some of the worst golf I have ever witnessed. Their names will never be found on winners trophies or displayed for all to see on the walls of the clubhouse but they are winners in many other ways. They win because they are the backbone of the membership. They enter competitions knowing they are unlikely to win the prizes. They put their names on lists for team selection knowing as they write, that they have an extremely slim chance of being selected, except for a shortage of better players being available. If you are such a player reading this take heart; to me you are a winner. In life it is no different, for the vast majority of us will never see ourselves as being that important or especially successful, but we all have the opportunity to influence our world, no matter how big or small that world may be.

A word of encouragement, a smile, giving someone your time, or a listening ear, although not valued in financial terms, can be worth more to one person than you may ever realise. John enjoyed his golf, and although he was not a well man, such an inconvenience could not stop him from participating in all manner of competitions and fun events. Being a totally honest player he would never seek to gain an advantage by incorrect scoring or by bending the rules. I never saw John angry or upset, except on one occasion when he knew that one of his opponents in a match play competition, sought to gain an advantage by (in John's own words) cheating. I will not go into the details, but the incident upset John enough as to make him very angry and he subsequently lost the match.

"Why did he do that?" John asked me as we spoke in the bar a couple of days after the incident. "Why do people go out and cheat? - because that's what you call it!" he continued. Now I know, human nature being what it is, you would really like to know what happened. I will simply say it involved a lost ball which on being found was not, as John claimed, the original ball hit. Having a competitive attitude on the course is one thing, but cheating in any form is not acceptable. It is possible for anyone, especially if they are not concentrating, to miss the little chip or the extra putt they took when adding up their score (especially if they took an eight or nine on a hole or have had a senior moment). But why do some players drop balls in the rough, trample down grass to improve their approach to the ball, tee up on fairways, kick their ball out of hazards and do whatever it takes to gain an advantage? It is said that you can tell more about a person's character on a golf course than anywhere else in life. I have known players banned for cheating and others suspended.

This is not confined to golf. In all competitive sport you will always find players or coaches who are willing to risk being caught in order to enhance the possibility of winning. In athletics much has been made of those who have taken performance-enhancing drugs. Cricket has had its off-field match fixing investigations, rugby has been in the headlines over players faking injury and other sports have had tragic stories of men and women taking or trying anything to gain an advantage.

I have a very good friend of mine called Arthur who is now retired, but in his prime he was the British, European, Commonwealth and World Powerlifting Champion and still holds world records for his amazing ability. He told me that he had witnessed, on more than one occasion, lifters who were so pumped up with drugs they didn't know what day it was.
He has seen guys walk on stage, walk past the weights they were supposed to lift, and walk off the stage all in one movement. Some were so pumped up with drugs that their hearts had ballooned which resulted in an early grave. We all have our own opinions regarding those who cheat on the sports field by breaking the rules or who try to gain an unfair advantage. John obviously was very angry when it happened to him and he vowed never to play with that member ever again.

The one thing which concerned me in writing this chapter was the thought that I had also met many people who had broken or bent the rules of everyday life. It may not have been a major sin like murder. It may be something much smaller, but nonetheless we have all broken the rules in life and I learnt that lesson when I was very young.

Friday afternoons were the only time I enjoyed my early years at school. Sports were on the timetable and I looked forward to that afternoon more than any other during the week. However 'blackmail' was on the timetable on Friday mornings. OK, it wasn't listed as such, but every Friday morning we were tested on some teaching or spelling or maths we had learnt during the week. If anyone did not achieve the required pass mark, Friday afternoon was spent in the classroom and not on the sports field. It was officially called revision but on reflection I called it 'blackmail.'

I remember well a couple of incidents at my primary school. One incident was on a Friday morning I had failed to reach the standard for spelling and needed to spell one word correctly if I was to enjoy football that afternoon. The word was 'received' and I struggled to get that one right. Outside the weather was perfect for football and after all these years I can still remember the day I kept going back to the teacher. "Sir is it r-e-c-e-v-e?" "No", he replied. I tried again, "Sir, how about r-i-c-e-v-e-e-d?" I confess I was guessing by then. "No", he replied again. It was now ten minutes before sports began and I had spent my lunch time learning and re-learning, when finally I met him again, "Sir, is it r-e-c-e-i-v-e-d?" I can still feel myself sweating over it now. "Yes, well done lad, go and get changed" he replied. Like a spring lamb I skipped down to the changing room while at the same time expressing my verbal approval to all who were in ear shot, YES! YES! YES! I did it.

I loved that word 'r-e-c-e-i-v-e-d'. I was so thrilled I grabbed my football boots, which in those days had solid toe caps, and swung them over my head with so much enthusiasm that a lace broke. I froze, and with a look of total shock and unbelief, I watched as my boot, which by now had changed into a missile, crashed through a very large (and I mean very large) window. I had also learned to spell t-r-o-u-b-l-e and I met it that afternoon as I was banned from the sports field.

I seemed to find trouble quite readily at school and the second incident took place when some lads jumped over a wall to chase a horse. The headmaster was livid. He came out, rounded us up and marched us into the main hall where he used the cane to great effect. "Sir, I didn't go over the wall, I was only watching." My last minute plea made no difference as I felt the full weight of the cane across my hand. As I walked along the pavement to my home, my hand was still very sore where the cane had done its work, but to avoid any further possibility of punishment for having the cane at school, I decided to keep quiet. I'm not sure if I had broken the rules as such by swinging my football boot around but I thought the lads must have done by chasing a horse and leaving the school grounds if my wounds had anything to go by.

A couple of days later I was once more walking back along that same pavement. Sunday had arrived and it was time for Sunday school. The wounds on my flesh had almost disappeared, but the deep wounds in my heart remained. I was a ten year old kid and even though I had grown up with the possibility of receiving a clip around the ear at home, my first cane experience (yes more were to follow), left me fearful and shocked from the experience. As I walked those last few paces toward the Sunday school building I was not looking forward to meeting my teacher who, in my case, was the same man who had punished me only a couple of days before.

Nothing was said on that morning or any other and I soon came to realise that school days and Sundays were to remain, in the eyes of some, independent of one another. So what happened on school days Monday to Fridays had no bearing whatsoever on what happened at Sunday school and visa versa, or so it seemed.

As I grew older I learnt about the justice system and crime and punishment. I had considered a career in law at one stage in my life and had spent a couple of years working hard on the subject until my vocation took another turn a few years later. Most people understand the principle behind crime and punishment or I should say 'justice'. We have all witnessed people on television demanding justice for a crime that somebody has committed. We have also witnessed tears and deep emotions when it appears to some that an inappropriate punishment had been given for a crime. John, rightly had a really deep feeling of injustice when his opponent cheated his way into the next round of a club knock out. Some may say "It's only a game for goodness sake; it's not that important." That may be true, but more important than the game or the result itself was the fact that someone had allegedly sought to gain an unfair advantage by cheating. When cheats are caught, most of us are happy to see justice done through suspension from the club or whatever action those in authority decide.

Just as golf has its rules and regulations, many years ago God handed Moses His rules for the way he would have us live. I am not surprised therefore that many of the laws in our justice system came originally from God. God's laws, called 'The Ten Commandments', are not a simple request, but a command from God for all to live by. In addition, God has declared that when His laws are broken, His justice would need to be satisfied. I am not looking to belittle anyone here, but it may be possible that you never knew God had written His Ten Commandments of life, so here they are in simplified form as taken from the Bible.

1. Do not worship any other gods.
2. Do not make any idols of any kind or bow down to any man-made idol or image.
3. Do not misuse the name of the Lord (blaspheme).
4. Remember the Sabbath day and keep it holy.
5. Honour your parents.
6. Do not murder.
7. Do not commit adultery.
8. Do not steal.
9. Do not testify falsely (lie).
10. Do not covet anything anyone else owns.

The Jewish leaders in Jesus' day were full of pride and would boast before Jesus of how righteous they were. Therefore, it was no wonder Jesus made so many angry when He called them 'whitewashed walls', meaning they looked good on the outside but on the inside they were totally unclean. He made it even more challenging by saying that if they were angry with another without cause, it's no different to God than murdering them, or if they looked at a woman with lust in their hearts, it was no different to God than committing adultery. The religious leaders simply ignored His claims and wrote Him off as a rebel who blasphemed God. Consequently they looked for every opportunity to get rid of Jesus.

The Bible says that we have all broken the rules. And if we're honest we have to agree.
Thankfully God did not leave it there. Even though we have broken His laws he has made away for us to be forgiven. Our slate can be wiped clean.

God declared that He would provide a means of escape for mankind from the terrible day of judgement that would come upon the world. That means of escape would come only through His Son Jesus Christ. He would not only carry the weight of the sin of the whole world upon Himself but the full punishment for man's sin.

Isaiah, an Old Testament prophet, wrote this of Jesus: "He was wounded and crushed for our sins. He was beaten that we may have peace. He was whipped, and we were healed! All of us like sheep have gone astray. We have left God's path to follow our own. Yet the Lord laid on Him the guilt and sins of us all." John, who wrote his Gospel in the New Testament, recorded these words of Jesus: "God so greatly loved and dearly prized the world that He gave up His only Son, so that whoever believes in Him shall not perish, but have eternal life." (John 3:16)

I know my friend John was upset when he believed that his playing partner had broken the rules, but I have tried to show in this chapter that in the heart of all of us lies the same problem. I learned a long time ago that Christianity isn't for perfect people. It was never intended for those who regarded themselves as being perfect. You wouldn't book an appointment to see a doctor or a consultant if you knew that you had perfect health. Yes, being a Christian is precisely for those who know that they are not perfect. If that is you, then you will be pleased to know God has provided a remedy for your condition.

Chapter Six
YOU ARE DISQUALIFIED

As I drove into the Merlin car park, sun rays were pouring through the car window, the air was still and I had one of those feelings that it was going to be a great day for golf. As I got out of the car, I could see that around the first tee, many golfers were gathered as they watched their fellow competitors teeing off. There seemed to be a buzz in the air. I'm not sure if it was because of the great weather we had that day or because it was competition day which always brought its own sense of excitement. I joined them for a few minutes and watched the normal array of shots you usually find amongst the average club golfer. A number of balls finished up in the driving range and a few others in the newly constructed pond which was well placed to catch, what would need to be, a rather wayward shot. The usual friendly banter was given and received as I walked into the clubhouse to meet up with Brian and Steve who were my team mates for the day.

Steve was sitting up at the bar enjoying a drink, which was his normal position before a round, while Brian was sitting at a table enjoying a snack, which was his normal position. The usual greetings followed and it wasn't long before we were standing on the first tee. "Have a good game" Steve said as we began our round. The normal handshakes took place as we convinced each other that this was going to be our day and we were going to 'burn up' the course. We had entered a Texas Scramble, a three man team competition which is hard enough to explain to the novice club golfer, let alone the non-golfer who may be reading this book. It is sufficient to say that the three of us played very well as a team and we were pleased with our score as we came off the last green.

Handshakes, smiles and the customary pat on the back with the 'well played guys' followed as we walked off the course and back into the clubhouse. One of the hidden rules in golf competitions is to keep your score under cover, especially if you know you have played well, until all the scores are in and the club captain or his representative announces the result. However it wasn't too long before it was known we had played very well and posted a good score. The committee and management decided to organise a ram roast following the golf, and soon we were having a bite to eat while reflecting on the possibility that we may have played well enough to be in the prizes.

I have known Steve for a number of years. He is a great guy, totally underestimated in ability and character but one of the backbone members of the club. He is an average player just like the majority of us but I have always believed that it is far more important to be a great guy who plays golf than a great golfer who isn't a great guy. I have come to admire his love and support for his family which was obvious to me one Saturday when Steve introduced them to me at the clubhouse. His lovely daughter ongoing health problems, but Steve introduced her with pride in his heart. This was his daughter and Steve's love for her was both strong and sincere. We soon finished our snack and knowing I had a busy Sunday the following day, I decided to make my way home.

I was soon relaxing in my bath enjoying a long hot soak. At such times I would often close my eyes and reflect on the round of golf just played. I very rarely got past the first six holes before dropping off in the bath and having a well earned rest. This Saturday evening was no different than most and as I awoke the water was now lukewarm. Within a few minutes I was out, dried and dressed for the evening.

The golf was now far behind me as I turned my thoughts to the sermon I would be preaching the next day. If we were in the prizes I knew that Steve would be still at the club ready to pick up any prize we had won, therefore when my phone rang, I was surprised to hear the voice of the club captain on the other end of the phone. "Hello," he said. "Is that Matt?" "Yes" I replied. "I understand you had a good round this afternoon, it looks like the team you were in finished second." "That's good" I said. "Matt we can't find your card, where is it?" In a moment I knew. I closed my eyes in disbelief as I realised that I had forgotten to hand it in. In the middle of the excitement of playing a good team round, then the ram roast and the general chatter, I had placed the card in my back pocket and had forgotten to take it out and hand it in. I explained what had happened to Ted, the club captain and thankfully he didn't spare the pain for too long. "I'm sorry Matt but you're disqualified."

I put the phone down and slumped back into my chair. My first thought was for Brian and Steve who had played so very well. What would they say? And it wasn't long before I found out as the phone rang. "You stupid so-and-so!" said Steve as I answered the phone. "Was that another senior moment? We were second until you forgot to put the card in!" Steve continued for a few moments longer and I could feel his disappointment as I apologised and the phone call ended. Looking at my notes for the next mornings meeting I reminded myself that the topic included the importance of forgiveness as a means of personal growth. I must admit I did think about having a bit of fun by posting Steve a copy, but wisdom prevailed.

Being disqualified from a round of golf is one thing, but my heart goes out to those who, through no fault of their own, experience social disqualification because of some inability or disability. I am so thankful that Merlin Golf Club was founded on the principle of inclusion for all. It was the intention of Ross and Margaret to provide golf for the everyday man and woman. Some of the heroes at Merlin are those who will never win a monthly medal, in fact they may never make a 'birdie' or break a hundred. However, they are there entering as many competitions as possible, knowing their chances of winning are slim, but they carry one simple truth; they are members and they belong.

As I look into the eyes of those who are rejected in life or who have received exclusion because they don't fit into the ideals of another, I cry out with my whole heart to remind them that they do belong. They belong to this great family of mankind. They belong and they have an important part to play out on the stage of life. I encourage them to take their place, to dream the impossible and to become someone bigger than the image others have placed upon them.

If the Christian message was about our own personal achievement, being religious in action and in deed and judging ourselves against the family next door, then we have missed the whole point of what Christianity is all about. It was the religious leaders who rejected Christ as He exposed the unfair and unrighteous demands they placed upon others. It was the religious leaders who would not accept Jesus as the Saviour of the world simply because He didn't fit into their ideals. Jesus went around proclaiming a message of love and inclusion for all. He went to those disqualified by the religious system and invited them to be His followers. One of His first messages was in the synagogue at Nazareth where He declared that the Holy Spirit had anointed Him to preach the good news to the poor; to those who knew that they were spiritually bankrupt. He declared that He had come to release the captives and to open the eyes of the blind. He declared that broken hearts would be mended and that the time for God's favour had come. The result was for the religious, legalistic leaders of Nazareth to take Him out and to try and throw Him over a cliff. Jesus however slipped away and they could not find Him.

Jesus went to Matthew, a tax collector , and simply said "Follow me." Matthew left all and followed him. The significance of this is that in truth Matthew would never have picked himself as one of the disciples of Jesus. As a tax collector he was totally excluded, by both the Romans because he was a Jew, and by his own people because he was working against them for an enemy power. So what was Jesus doing picking him? He was showing us all that the Kingdom of God is not an exclusive zone for perfect individuals (if ever you could find such a person). The Kingdom of God is not reserved for a special few. All can be included, however the way in is by a personal invitation. Jesus still invites, he is still speaking, calling and encouraging all to follow him.

Brian, who would have described himself as not the happiest person on earth, would have quickly disqualified himself from any thought or possibility of being included in God's family. However Brian was on God's invitation list. Although I only knew Brian from a distance, his journey towards Jesus began one Tuesday morning at the golf club. Bill, one of the original senior members of the club knew something of my work and approached me as I was sitting enjoying a coffee. "Brian" he said, "isn't very good. He's in the changing room and very upset, do you think you could have a word?" Bill had hardly finished speaking when I saw Brian approaching. He looked tired, was unshaven and quite frankly looked troubled.

"Morning Brian, can you spare a couple of minutes"? I said, and soon we were sitting in the dining room at Merlin. "Bill was just saying that he thought you were quite upset in the changing room; can I help in any way?" "Don't know" he replied. "It's my son - he is in hospital in Truro and in quite a bad way. I'm not sure if he will get through and if he does he may have some serious ongoing problems. I didn't know what to do, I just had to get out of the house and talk to somebody." "Well here I am and you're talking to somebody now, so keep talking" I said.

Brian continued to pour out his heart, explaining what had happened to his son, an issue that I have not included as it is quite private, but it is sufficient to say all was not well. "I will be praying for him and for you all as a family", I assured him. Brian simply replied that he would be praying also. That evening at one of our fellowship evenings at home with a group of friends we prayed, as promised.

The next time I saw Brian he was overjoyed. "Oh prayer works! It's fantastic! Peter is home and he has no ongoing problems! Thank you for praying, and I prayed as well", he said with obvious delight. A few days later I was travelling with him to Cape Cornwall to play in one of our senior golf matches. As we travelled together he was full of questions about my faith and God. I was soon explaining that Christianity was not about having a religion based on good works. I continued to share with him, explaining that Christianity was all about having personal relationship with God through Jesus Christ.

A few seconds passed before Brian responded in a quiet, yet thoughtful manner, "God would never accept me; I'm disqualified and I would never be good enough for him. There is no way I could ever become a Christian." I have heard those same words many times over from all manner of people, no matter their background or their upbringing. It mattered not if they were poor or rich, powerful or not. Some admitted that they were not perfect, but that they had tried to be a good person; perhaps even feeling that they were no worse than anyone else. Others however, felt completely disqualified.

"Brian, none of us are good enough. We have all sinned and we have all fallen short of God's standards." "Well I guess that disqualifies all of us," Brian replied. "Yes, you're right," I said.

By now we arrived at Cape Cornwall to play our match. Cape Cornwall cannot be any further west; the course is at times almost on the cliff edge with some of the most wonderful scenes anywhere in the world. There wasn't a cloud in the sky as we walked out on to the first tee. The air was clean, the sea was a beautiful deep blue and even the breakers of the surf rolled in a lazy manner as they broke over the cliff face. In the distance a few people were walking slowly on the cliff path and nothing or no one seemed to want to rush the moment or the day. This was the day to play golf. The day when records could be broken. Everything felt perfect as I placed my ball on the tee. The green in the distance looked inviting as I selected my six iron, addressed the ball and played my shot.

The fact that it landed nowhere near the green and that my round went from bad to worse made no difference to the enjoyment of the day. We were soon travelling home and it wasn't long before we were once more talking about how it was possible to know God in such an intimate way.

"Do you know about Jesus being crucified on a cross"? I asked. Brian simply said that he did but thought it was because Jesus was a radical and went around upsetting the political system. I explained that the cross was the place where God demonstrated his love for all of us. I explained to Brian how God so loved each one of us that He gave his only Son as a sacrifice for our sin. Jesus blood was shed. His death for our life, so that we may not perish but have everlasting life. Jesus said Himself that He did not come into the world to condemn us, but that through Him we might be saved. I explained to Brian that although we are all guilty of sin and are disqualified from eternal life in Heaven, Jesus became God's sacrifice for our sin as He laid down His life on the cross. This qualifies all who come to Him and ask for His forgiveness. We are not qualified by anything we do on our part. We are qualified simply by coming to Jesus and receiving by faith His gift of eternal life.

The next few miles were very quiet and it was only broken when Brian finally spoke, "Well I certainly need to think about what you are saying. Can we talk again?"

The following Sunday afternoon I was sitting in Brian's fish and chip shop. A few customers were tucking into and obviously enjoying their meal. It had been a while since I sat surrounded by that unique smell in the air that only a fry-up can create. I was tempted when Brian asked "Do you want something to eat? I have some really lovely cod in the fryer, you know it's beautiful and the chips are something else!"

It wasn't difficult to see that Brian had, what he called, a quality control relationship with his shop. I'm not sure if I had ever seen anyone light up in talking about food as Brian did on that Sunday afternoon. Having just had a meal at home I resisted the offer and settled for a mug of coffee which was most welcome.

"Brian, have you thought about our last conversation?" I asked as I began to sip my second cup of coffee. "Yes mate, I have given it a lot of thought and although I don't understand everything, I can see that I need Jesus in my life. What do I do?"

For the next few minutes I once again explained that being a Christian wasn't about trying to become religious or living under a set of rules. I once more explained that it was all about the restoration of a living relationship between God and each of us individually; a relationship which was originally broken because of man's rejection of God, yet restored through the sacrifice of Jesus. This, I explained was God's love and justice expressed in a single act.

"Do you mean to say that Jesus, God's Son, died on a cross for my sin?" Brian asked. "Yes Brian. Simply put, He took your place. He died so that we may live and receive God's gift of eternal life." "OK what do I need to do?" he asked. I sipped another mouthful of coffee from the mug as I reflected on the reason why I was here, not just in Brian's shop, but my own personal calling to be a bridge between Jesus and all who would look for him. Knowing God is a wonderful experience and having the joy of introducing another to God made me very excited. I sat opposite Brian as I had sat opposite many people before, thinking of the special moment that was about to happen.

"Brian you simply receive God's salvation as you would receive any other gift. You can't earn it; you just receive It. Would you like me to lead you in a very simple prayer, asking for God's forgiveness and for Jesus to become the Lord of your life?" "Yes, now, right here, I'm ready!" Brian replied.

All around us people were still eating, plates were being cleared, customers were coming and going, but in the midst that chip shop there were three people sat at one table. Brian, myself and God. We made that little table a meeting house for the three of us and we were not ashamed or embarrassed as we prayed:

"Jesus come into my heart and forgive me for all my sins. I receive your gift of life and salvation, amen" Brian prayed. The room, by now was filled with a different kind of aroma; the very presence of God brought sweetness and a calmness over the face of Brian as he looked up. I'm not sure if there was a tear in his eye, but I know there was one in mine. "Wow, that was fantastic; I'm a Christian!" were Brian's first words. "You are" I replied. Brian didn't know what to say or how to react to this freedom he was beginning to experience. Nor could he explain the strange yet warm presence that filled his life.

Now as I looked at the un-submitted score card which I had pulled from my back pocket, I thought about how pleased I was that Brian had started a new life. "Well Brian" I said to myself, "Forgiveness is about to be the first subject you will learn as a new Christian."
Being disqualified from a round of golf is not a major problem. It may be disappointing for an hour or two but at the bottom line it is only a game. If someone is socially excluded because of their race, colour, ability or inability, or for any other reason, that is a far greater tragedy. To look down on another is the lowest point of humanity. My greatest concern is for all people everywhere who are currently excluded from the Kingdom of God. I am concerned for those who have never entered into a living fellowship with God through Jesus Christ. I am concerned at the inability of the Christian Church to communicate the importance of a personal salvation for all. It is possible to live a good life, to do your best for mankind, to be religious in behaviour and still be disqualified from the greatest gift anyone can receive; the gift of eternal life.

Thankfully God has provided a way for all to be included.

Chapter Seven

A GAME FOR ALL

November 16th 2004 opened a new chapter in my golfing life as I joined Merlin Seniors for the first time. "Just a moment everyone, before we tee off I want to introduce Matt our latest senior member." "Not yet for another week," I replied. Dan and the rest would have none of that as they simply said "One week won't make any difference so get your clubs. We are playing an individual Stableford, full handicap." I soon realised that seniors golf was an entirely different game than I was used to playing. The rule book had been changed by some players or perhaps never actually read. Some could not count or remember the number of shots played, and players of a certain age would disappear quite frequently in the trees or behind the hedge to answer nature's call. Arthur who was in his early sixties had a word in my ear, "Now listen Matt, you won't be going around here in three hours and you will need a lot of patience at times."

I would not regard myself as a big hitter (although I can compete with any average player for distance) but the first morning I played with two seniors I had a bit of a shock as Arthur's words came back to me. The third at Merlin is a par 5 and with favourable conditions it is very possible to reach the green in two. I had a following wind as I hit the ball sweet and I knew it had travelled a long way. A six iron for my next shot and I would be putting for an eagle. Both of my playing partners were quite elderly and both had full handicaps of 28.

"Where did that go?" asked one partner as I walked off the tee area. "Down the fairway, middle left" I replied. I then watched them both tee off and to my amazement one just reached the ladies tee and the other hit the ball about 50 yards. "Good shot," said one as he walked to his ball still sitting on the ladies tee. "Thanks," said the other. I walked with them as they both produced an array of shots that you would never find in the coaching books.

After both players had played about three shots, one turned to me and asked, "Have you given up on this hole, is your ball lost?" "No, we haven't reached it yet," I replied. "It's about another 50 yards or so, but we are almost there." As I looked up I noticed the group in front of us were equally as slow and were only walking on to the green to putt out. My playing partners had now played about five shots as we reached my ball. I took out my 6 iron and proceeded to wait until the green cleared. "What are you waiting for?" asked one of the other players. "Oh, just waiting for the green to clear," I replied, and without another word I hit a decent shot to within eight feet of the pin. "What a shot, wow! What's your handicap? You must be a professional!" and other questions followed.

I assured them I was not that good and I confirmed the same only ten minutes later as I drove my tee shot on the 4th straight out of bounds! One of my player partners gave me a slight smile before he said, "Aw, you're only trying to make us feel better."

The rest of the round took over four hours to complete. My playing partners had no reason to be in a hurry; after all they were retired. Golf for them was to be enjoyed and the occasional good shot was a bonus. For them a par was as rare as winning the lottery while a 5 on the card was fantastic. I really enjoyed my first experience playing with the seniors and through it I discovered that this game was for all to enjoy irrespective of ability. We shook hands on the 18th green and I was pleased with my 38 points. By the time we walked into the clubhouse, most of the players had gone home except those who thought they may be in with a shout of winning on the day.

"Hi Matt" said Dan. "How did you enjoy it? Did you have a good day?" I handed him my card and he looked at it quite intently for a little while. "38 points, well you have won it, the next best is 35." Dan thought for a moment before he added, "Obviously seeing you're not a senior until next week, you can't be in the prizes." "Of course" I added, "I fully understand."

Within a couple of years, I was invited by Neil to follow him as the Senior Captain. I accepted and the next twelve months really convinced me that golf was a game for all irrespective of age or ability. Over that year I tried to play with as many senior members as possible. Often I would need to point out some of the basic rules and interpretations of the laws of the game. Unfortunately, this wasn't always appreciated. One member informed me that golf was fun before I became captain. "We could just turn up and play without worrying about it. You're making it all too serious!" he remonstrated. I had just informed him that taking a drop from behind a hazard did not mean picking the ball up and throwing it thirty feet on to the fairway!

Keith was a great help by arranging all our matches against other clubs, on a home-and-away basis. All these games were played in the right spirit, but there were times when I raised my eyebrows in shock or unbelief. I was surprised how serious some of the players, especially from other clubs, acted during those friendly matches.

During one very close match which was tied, I asked my host players if I could drive my ball over a hedge as the fairway was a dog-leg to the right. I had never played the course before and I wasn't sure if such a shot was sensible. "You can if you want," he replied. Having hit my drive to cut the corner my host, without moving an inch from his previous position, simply said "Good shot, but it's out of bounds over that hedge." "I thought you said it was ok for me to play that shot!" I protested to which he replied, "No you only asked me if it was ok to drive your ball over that hedge. Well you can drive it where you like, but you didn't ask me if that hedge was out of bounds".

The rest of the match was played in relative silence.

I remember thinking as I drove home of the foolishness of such behaviour. At a time in life when all should be grateful for having the health and strength to walk around a golf course, meet new players and enjoy the moment, it was disappointing to find such an attitude. The truth is, age doesn't always change character or attitude and growing old gracefully doesn't apply as much as it ought, especially when it comes to competitive golf matches.

Perhaps the worst experience I had of unbelievable behaviour (and to my regret it was the only time I refused to shake hands with another player at the end of a round) happened at one of our home matches. The weather that day was wet and windy, and I mean it was gusting to 60 or 70 mph! Our 10th is a generous par 5, but on this day we were playing straight into the face of a storm. I remember hitting my driver well, then a three wood twice, and I had still not reached the 150 yard marker! A four iron followed which still left a chip to the green. The other players were struggling as much as I was to reach the green and when we all finally arrived I declared that I was on for five and asked how many shots the others in the group had taken. Turning to one of my opponents I was shocked (in fact I laughed) when he said "two." "No, not a two. That's impossible, think again!" I said as we walked onto the green. I turned to his playing partner who had played some good shots, "How many have you played?" "Seven" he replied. "Well your mate claims he has only played two," I said. No answer came and I watched as the 'two' golfer three putted, walked off the green and claimed a five. Thankfully because of the wind and rain, the match was called off by the time we played the next hole.

Now don't get me wrong. I don't mind if we win or lose provided the game is played fairly and in the right spirit. Once again I found myself asking, "Why?" I soon answered it by reminding myself that golf is played by all kinds of people no matter what ability or character they might have.

Yes we all play at different levels and one of my most enjoyable times was when I played a match with my good friend Derek. Derek has a handicap of 28, this was his first handicap and I would be surprised, as would Derek, if it dropped much lower. That is not meant to be disrespectful it is just the reality of the level to which Derek plays. He is now well into his seventies and keeps very fit. He enjoys his golf and the fellowship of the other members. Tee to green, Derek plays well but around the greens I have seen Derek look totally frustrated at his difficulty in reading a putt. Derek doesn't play in the matches against other clubs so I was delighted when he accepted my invitation to be my partner against one of the clubs we entertained. We played well together but Derek was still struggling around the greens. He played the 13th well and as I had already lost my ball I knew my contribution was over. Derek faced a very tricky down hill putt of about 20 feet to keep us in the match. He looked determined and I looked downcast.

Suddenly the ball was on its way. "It's going to be close" I thought, when suddenly it took a break and dropped into the hole. Derek's expression never changed, he simply walked over to the hole, took out his ball and walked to the next tee. That hole was the beginning of a sudden change of form. We won the next three holes and soon the game was over. Derek's putt had set us on the road to victory.

Everyone who plays this game will have wonderful moments when they will play a shot or two as well as a professional. The rest of the shots or putts may not be worth talking about. Such was Derek's experience on that special day. Just as golf is an inclusive sport, available to all, I cannot finish this chapter without saying the same about the

Kingdom of God. If the Kingdom of God was compared to the finest golf course ever, then Jesus came to make membership available to everyone, no matter what handicap they may carry or whatever their own personal ability. Most, if not all would do one of two things:

1) They would think they could never afford to be members of such a course.
2) Some may feel that it is only reserved for a few special people.

The majority of Jesus' time on this earth was spent inviting those who were excluded by the religious system into the Kingdom of God. The poor in spirit, the sick, those who regarded themselves as needing salvation, He came to them all. He sat with publicans and sinners. He allowed a prostitute to weep at His feet as she looked for mercy.

In His own words He said, "I have come that you may have life and have it to the full." There is no doubt Jesus came with a purpose and that simply was to stand in the gap between God and man and make a way for reconciliation. I once heard a story of a young lad who had turned to a life of crime in the town where he lived. He was poor and it wasn't long before he found himself before the local judge to answer for his crimes. He pleaded guilty and in order for justice to be met the young man was ordered to pay a rather hefty fine or go to prison. What the young man didn't know was that the judge recognised the name and the address of this young offender as being the home of a very good friend he had known a few years previously. Circumstances had taken these two good friends apart; one continued his law studies while the other, through redundancy and sickness had fallen on hard times.

The judge had a dilemma; justice had to be met but he knew that this young offender and his family could not pay the fine. Once the judge pronounced the fine, he saw the shock on the face of the offender and it was obvious he had no idea what was awaiting him. Then something quite remarkable took place, the judge took off his official robes walked over to the clerk of the court and wrote out a cheque for the full amount. He turned to the young man and said "You are free; the price is paid."

That is the message Jesus not only taught, but made possible by taking off His royal attire, becoming a man, paying the price for our freedom that we may all go free. Free from the final judgement of God and free in knowing that we have been totally pardoned of all our sins. Yet, as the young offender could not go free until he accepted the gift of grace from the Judge, we cannot go free until we also come to Jesus and accept His gift of grace.

When Jesus was once reclining at a table enjoying a meal, he illustrated this wonderful gift of grace as he spoke to the man who invited him. "When you put on a lunch or a dinner, don't invite friends, brothers, relatives, and rich neighbours. For they will repay you by inviting you back. Instead, invite the poor, the crippled, the lame, and the blind. Then at the resurrection of the godly, God will repay you." Hearing this, a man sitting at the table with Jesus exclaimed, "What a privilege it would be to have a share in the Kingdom of God!"

Jesus replied with this illustration: "A man prepared a great feast and sent out many invitations. When all was ready, he sent his servant around to notify the guests that it was time for them to come. But they all began making excuses. One said he had just bought a field and wanted to inspect it, so he asked to be excused. Another said he had just bought five pair of oxen and wanted to try them out. Another had just been married, so he said he couldn't come. The servant returned and told his master what they had said. His master was angry and said, 'Go quickly into the streets and alleys of the city and invite the poor, the crippled, the lame and the blind.' After the servant had done this, he reported, 'there is still room for more.' So his master said, 'Go out into the country lanes and behind the hedges and urge anyone you find to come, so that the house will be full. For none of those I invited first will get even the smallest taste of what I had prepared for them.' "

As golf is a game for all abilities and for all people, so is the Kingdom of God. The price has been paid; the invitation is going out. YOU ARE INVITED!

I make no apology for repeating this theme.
The only question is, "will you accept the invitation?"

Chapter Eight

NEVER TOO LATE

I watched in total silence, as Bill stood over one of the most challenging putts of his entire golfing life. To me, it looked a straight forward four to five feet slightly uphill putt which on a normal day would not cause any problem. Today however, was not a normal day and if the putt ahead of Bill would have won the Ryder Cup for Europe, it would not have been more important to him. For the first time in the round, I noticed a slight tension in his face, although his eyes were fixed on the task before him. This was his opportunity. This was his moment. But was this to be his hour?

I noticed a slight twitch in his hands as he gripped his club. He released his hands and gripped again, another glance at the hole and the ball was on its way. There was no gallery, and a passing motorist, who may have glanced in our direction, would have had no idea whatsoever of the drama that was unfolding before him on the 17th green. This was Bill's opportunity at the age of 80, bar a few days, to win his first major golf competition; the Brian Linzey Seniors Knock out Cup. He had reached the final by beating some useful golfers and I had reached the final a few weeks earlier having had a good tussle with Steve in the semi-final. Bill and sport had been constant companions throughout his life. He played darts for Cornwall and also played cricket in the Cornwall first division.

Although Bill kept himself very fit, he had a heart attack in his sixties and was advised to watch his diet and to exercise. He started to play golf intermixed with regular walking and it wasn't long before he became well and totally committed to this new found sport. Bill, when most guys his age are quite content to plod around in the greenhouse and enjoy the occasional cup of cocoa, is still very competitive. My first encounter of 'Competitive Bill' took place one Tuesday (which is Senior's day at Merlin) while we were playing in a three man team competition.

Our team was standing on the 14th tee as Bill and his team were approaching the green on the 13th. I had one of those 'senior' moments and without thinking I teed off from the white marker instead of the yellow. The white was about nine feet behind the yellow. My two companions followed my mistake and suddenly I heard Bill now on the 13th green shout across, "You're all disqualified, wrong tee!"

We carried on with our round, but not much golf was played as my two playing partners lost heart and the desire to continue. "Come on chaps, its not the end of the world. We have played nine feet more than the rest! I'm sure the captain won't disqualify us for that slight error, it's only a fun day after all." "You don't know Bill," they said "he's strict when it comes to the rules and will make his point known". Technically they were right, but thankfully our score did not suggest there would be any confrontation in the clubhouse once the cards were submitted. I simply wrote disqualified over the card as I handed it to the captain, adding; PLAYED OFF WRONG TEE in large letters. Although Bill expects all to play by the rules (and who can argue with that) he is a very well liked and respected member of Merlin. Together we have shared some very good times and some not so good.

A few months before we played in the final of the knockout, I attended the funeral of Bill's long term sweetheart and wife, Betty. Driving towards Truro, I was not surprised to find a queue of cars trying to get to the car park of the crematorium. When I finally arrived, I was ushered to the far car park and was pleased to see Neil and Dan and a few other golfers from Merlin. A few minutes later we were in our seats, not far from Bill who looked very resilient. He reminded me of a good soldier who was determined to stay calm on the outside whilst full of emotion and pain on the inside. He had nursed Betty for many years; now finally she was out of pain and at rest.

As we filed out I noticed Peter, the same Peter who had welcomed me at Merlin on my first visit. It was good to see him again. Peter in true fashion tried to lift the atmosphere with a funny story, but on this occasion it didn't work. By now I could see Bill standing as one by one he thanked family and friends for attending. A handshake, a greeting and a few words; nothing more needed to be said. And yet suddenly as I stood before him I felt a deep empathy and I was able to feel the depth of his sorrow. I guess I broke the rules again as I put my arms around him and gave him a big hug.

"We are here for you Bill." "I know. Thanks" he replied.

As I moved away I noticed a few tears had formed not only in Bills eyes, but in mine also. Over the months that followed, Merlin became Bill's home as he allowed the activities and the members to be used to heal his pain, little by little. Our friendship grew and he and I were delighted when I won the Bill Scott Trophy back to back in 2007 and 2008. He used to say "The only reason I donated the Bill Scott Trophy was because I will never see my name on another one."

But was that about to change on the 17th as we played the final of the Brian Linzey Knock out cup? The putt was on the way and I felt I was in a win-win situation. If Bill had missed we would have gone down the last, and if the putt dropped, I would have been delighted that Bill had won. Suddenly the tension was over and Bill's face turned to shock and surprise as his ball dropped to the bottom of the cup. Motionless, he stood for a moment as though he had just been caught like a rabbit in car headlights.

I walked over and gave him a big hug. "Congratulations Bill, well done - you have won 2 and 1. Well played!" It was a few seconds before he spoke. "I can't believe I won. I won!" It was as though he was trying to convince himself. "Yes Bill, giving him another pat on the back, you won and I am delighted for you." Once more I detected a slight tear, but this time it was a tear of joy and not sorrow.

If I had given Bill a thousand pounds it wouldn't have made him happier than winning his first trophy. He had won at the age of 80 (less a few weeks), something he never thought possible. Bill was to celebrate his 80th birthday on October 28th and I knew just how much he was missing his wife and how he would have longed for Betty to be with him. I therefore decided to arrange a surprise for him. Thankfully he agreed to partner me on my senior's Captain's Day which we arranged to fall on his birthday.

While we were on the course, everything was organised, even down to Club Captain Mark arriving to present Bill with a year's free membership, thanks to the generosity of the Barlow family and the members. Bill and Tom were the last to arrive back to the clubhouse after our round. By now they were wet as the skies had opened on the 18th and it poured down. I made an excuse to cut my round short on the 16th and consequently I stayed totally dry! Tom almost carried Bill into the changing room making sure that he was not going to go anywhere near the lounge area. After a few minutes I joined Bill in the changing rooms.

"You knew when to come off the course!" said Bill. "Did you have some inside information? Tom and I were soaked." "Don't worry about that", I said. "I'm ready to present the prizes for today. Are you ready?" He combed his hair, or at least the two bits on the side, and joined me to walk the few yards to where the members were ready to meet him. I made sure he was taking the lead as we joined the others. Suddenly, as though some heavenly choir master had brought them in, the members began to sing "For He's A Jolly Good Fellow." Bill, thinking they were referring to me, as senior captain, looked to step aside and let me through.

"No Bill this is for you. Happy birthday!" I said as I placed my hand on his shoulder and encouraged him forward. The men continued to sing, "Happy birthday to you, happy birthday to you, happy birthday dear Bill, happy birthday to you!"

Suddenly I felt a surge of pride in those men as I somehow knew they meant every word they sung. Bill had difficulty staying composed as the raw emotion of that moment was etched on his face. Next, the presentations to those who had won prizes in the competition were made. Mark presented the gift of free golf membership for the following year and other keepsakes were given. Finally Bill was presented with one of the largest 'Superman' cakes you could ever imagine made by Linda. Speeches were made and Bill, now quite emotional, gave a wonderful reply.

A few days later I had the joy of presenting Bill with the Brian Linzey Knock Out Cup. As I handed the cup to him I was overjoyed. Not because he defeated me in the final, but because between us all, we were able to help Bill turn some tears of sorrow into tears of joy. Eighty year old Bill had won his first golf trophy and it was a day he would never forget. What made all the difference to Bill was the fact that he achieved, as far as he was concerned, what he thought was impossible.

The word 'impossible' is not one of my favourite words especially when it relates to God and the rest of us. Wally, who was not a golfer, was invited to a meeting I was taking one evening at Liskeard Christian Centre, now called Greenbank. This is his story: "My wife Sandra invited me to listen to the guy who was going to preach at her church. Normally when asked, I would tell her I wasn't interested in religion or anything like that. On this occasion however, I felt it was right to go and although I sat and listened I was determined that I wasn't going to let God get to me. I stood with the rest as the meeting came to an end. The worship band was playing a few songs as people moved forward for personal and individual prayer. I thought they obviously needed God but it wasn't for me. I was a tough guy. I had been a street fighter and I was very proud of the fact that no man had ever floored me. I was thinking that not even God could do that when suddenly I was hit with a power that was both full of love and strength. No one was around me, but the power of God was so strong it did what no man had ever done before, it floored me.

Lying on the floor, I was laughing for joy. At the same time I was weeping and asking for God's forgiveness as my stubborn pride had kept him out of my life. I thought I didn't need God but how wrong I was. My life was totally transformed and if anyone had asked me a few days earlier about me finding Christ, I would have said "Impossible!" But now I'm one of the happiest men on earth."

A few months later Wally with his wife and family moved to South America and although we kept in contact for a few months Wally's work took him away from home for weeks and months at a time and caused me to lose contact. One morning I received an email from Wally. He had news that he had developed cancer and his prognosis was not good. He asked us to pray for an impossible situation.

Well, now a couple of years later, I have just received another email from Wally. It reads; "Glory be to God! I am now cancer-free. It has totally baffled the doctors here. They cannot get their heads around the fact that such a big tumour can disappear without surgery. Surgery was not possible because the cancer had taken over and destroyed all the ducts in my liver which drained the poisons from my liver. All the specialists and doctors gave me between 8 to 12 months and here I am waiting to complete the job I know the Lord has me to do."

Wally has enjoyed at least two remarkable miracles. Both, he would have said, were impossible at one stage in his life. The first miracle was the transformation he experienced in knowing Jesus and the second was the healing of cancer in his body – praise God. For Wally it was not too late.

The oldest person I had the joy of introducing to a new life in Jesus was 92. He had attended church all his life, but never understood the message of the cross, until it was explained in easy to understand terms. In asking Jesus into his life and deciding to make God the centre of his remaining years, he left the meeting that morning rejoicing. In the natural he may have thought that at 92 it was impossible to start a new life, but he did!

I could write no small book on the joy I have had in seeing individuals finding a new purpose and direction for life when they have been reconciled to God. The Bible declares that there is much rejoicing in heaven over one person who repents and turns to God. It also speaks of a great feast when Jesus returns; a great wedding feast when all tears will be wiped away forever. When I look at the cross of Jesus, the place where the wrath of God was poured out, I have mixed emotions. I am obviously so pleased that I have found Christ and that his presence has been a continual source of delight to me for many years. I have had the joy and delight of preaching the wonderful message of salvation for over forty years. I have wept with the broken and rejoiced with those who have reached out to God and have found his promises to be true.

As I read and absorb the account of the crucifixion, I am filled with deep gratitude and emotion as I remember that

Jesus Christ died for me. His walk to Calvary, the nails that pierced Him and pinned Him to a piece of wood, the crown of thorns which was pressed into His head and the spear buried into His side; all cry out to remind me of the cost of my salvation. And yet, two others were crucified with Jesus one on His right and the other on His left. So what made the crucifixion of Jesus so different?

Isaiah, a prophet who prophesied of Jesus many hundreds of years before His birth, wrote this in regard to the suffering of the cross:

"He was despised and rejected - a man of sorrows, acquainted with deepest grief.
We turned our backs on Him and looked the other way when he went by.
He was despised, and we did not care.
Yet it was our weaknesses He carried;
it was our sorrows that weighed him down.
And we thought His troubles were a punishment was from God for His own sins!
But He was wounded and crushed for our sins.
He was beaten so we could be whole.
He was whipped so we could be healed.
All of us like sheep have strayed away.
We have left God's path to follow our own.
Yet the Lord laid on Him the sins of us all.
He was oppressed and treated harshly, yet He never said a word."

Luke, a doctor and one of the writers who recorded the crucifixion of Jesus wrote in regard to the two criminals who were crucified also;

"One of the criminals hanging beside him scoffed. "So you're the Messiah, are you? Prove it by saving yourself; and us too while you're at it." But the other criminal protested. "Don't you fear God even when you have been sentenced to die? We deserve to die for our crimes, but this man hasn't done anything wrong." Then he said "Jesus, remember me when you come into your Kingdom." And Jesus replied. "I assure you today you will be with me in paradise."

When I look at the cross I am faced with the reality that even in the midst of death, one criminal scoffed at Jesus. He represents many who scoff and laugh and openly mock Jesus today. In truth, nothing has changed for over 2000 years. Jesus Christ is still used as a swear word. Some, who are atheists, will work overtime to try and debunk the story of Jesus Christ. As I write these lines I am aware that in different parts of the world Christians are being persecuted and killed for proclaiming Jesus Christ, whilst others are in stinking prisons locked away behind bars, separated from their homes and families for preaching Christ.

One criminal represented many others when he said. "We deserve to die for our crimes, but this man has done nothing wrong. Remember me Jesus when you come into your Kingdom." This criminal left it late but as he called out to Jesus, Jesus reached out and declared "Today you will be with me in Paradise."

I have already said that in looking at the cross I have mixed emotions, emotions of great joy tinged with great sorrow. I have respect for all at the golf club both men and women, irrespective of who they are or where they have been.

I know Christ has paid a high price for their salvation. He has paid that same price for all who may be reading this book but have no idea of the difference between a 7 iron and a 3 wood. I am sorrowful because some have already declared to me that they have no time for God. Others have said that they feel they have gone too far and consequently God would never have them back.

I don't know what you may believe. I'm not sure, if you were present at the cross and heard the conversation of the two criminals, which one you would have stood with. But this I know: if Jesus was willing to forgive a criminal whose crime deserved death even near the end of his life, He is willing to forgive and save you. There is a trophy to win, a crown of life to receive; an inheritance reserved for you in Heaven and the promise of eternal life. It is never too late. While you still have breath in your body, God will not give up on you.

You can still win.
Just ask Bill.

Chapter Nine

NEW OWNERSHIP

"Have you heard Matt, they are going to sell the club!" said someone. "I heard it's going to be turned into a holiday park and the place will be covered in caravans, but they will keep nine holes for the holiday makers," said another. The rumours were coming thick and fast and I could tell that something was in the air. Ross, it appeared had lost interest in golf. His first love of horses had began to dominate his conversation over the previous months and a part of the complex was given over to building some stables. The course itself, whilst maintained, wasn't really going anywhere, in fact, in the eyes of the members, it had gone downhill. Some long term members had begun to leave and join other clubs and Merlin having started so well in its development, had ceased running the race and was limping rather slowly along. More than one member felt it was crisis time at Merlin. If we just continued to drift along, we would have lost more members, and in truth, we were not recruiting that many.

My opportunity came one Saturday morning. Cyril and I had played an early round and were back in the clubhouse. Ross was reading the papers and enjoying a coffee and the atmosphere was very relaxed.

"Morning Ross, nice one isn't it" I opened up the conversation. "Morning Matt, Cyril, you boys been out?"

"Yes, we had an early one this morning" I replied and I continued my conversation by asking him if there was any truth in the rumour that he was selling up. He gave a bit of a half smile as he thought over his reply but the good thing about Ross was that he was straight with you. More than one person had realised that there was no need to fill in the blanks following a conversation with Ross.

"Well there are a couple of people interested and it looks like one is very positive, but don't worry chaps it will remain as it is, I will make sure of that. I would rather sell it for a bit less and make sure Merlin remains as a golf course."

Nothing more was said. Nothing had to be said. Ross had spoken. Merlin was to be sold and Merlin would continue to provide golf. Margaret however remained very quiet over the forthcoming sale and it appeared to most of us that Margaret, who had invested a lot of time and energy into the development of Merlin, was not overjoyed at the prospect of selling her 'baby'. Of course the rumours did not go away, they just changed in nature. "It won't be so good once Margaret and Ross leave, it will be like losing your parents." said one. "You look out now; the membership fees will go sky high." "No matter, who buys it they will want to get their money back, and who will pay for that? Me and you, that's who!" said another, in a somewhat angry tone.

Within a few weeks, Merlin took on a cosmetic transformation. Suddenly old and rusted out machinery was being transported off site. The horses, which were not always popular with the members, were soon in their horse boxes as they left Merlin for the last time.

Once more the atmosphere changed from quiet anticipation at the expected arrival of the new owners, to a deep appreciation for all that Ross and Margaret had achieved in making it possible for a lot of people to begin playing golf, myself included. I don't think we had the opportunity to say goodbye to Ross and Margaret. The handover took place rather quickly once the contracts were signed. Perhaps they preferred it that way.

A few months later as Cyril and I were playing one Saturday morning, again quite early, I saw a lonely figure walking down the path which ran parallel to the 3rd fairway. Walking quite slowly and what appeared in a very contemplative manner he stopped occasionally and looked out across the course. Cyril broke the silence "That's Ross!"

It was so good to see him again. We stopped for a moment and exchanged pleasantries. You know what I mean, "Lovely day! Are you keeping well? How's Margaret?" Not too many words were spoken and I had the thought (rightly or not) that perhaps Ross was looking once more over the course that he had constructed to see how much had changed.

Changed it had. The new owners who also owned the luxury four star Budock Vean Hotel nestled in 65 acres of sub-tropical gardens and parkland on the banks of the tranquil Helford River, began an investment programme which changed every aspect of Merlin. A new head green keeper, affectionately known as 'Bear' by the members, was appointed who immediately set about the task of improving every aspect of the course.

Today Merlin has, through an incredible amount of dedication and hard work, become a beautiful heath-land golf course. Golfers from other clubs and the casual golfer are always full of praise for the state of the course, the friendliness of the clubhouse and the welcome they receive. It would be totally wrong to say that the new owners were content to tweak the changes. They were in no way interested in slight tweaking. They had bought Merlin and it was going to be improved and investment was going to be made.

When someone becomes a Christian, it may surprise you to learn that a transfer of ownership also takes place. Prior to coming to know Christ we are influenced by all manner of evil and sin that are in this world. We are slaves to our habits, our fears and our concerns. We can spend our whole life trying to find the 'magic formula' that finally gives that deep sense of peace, love, joy and happiness that in truth we all search for. When people tell me that they are their own boss, I do appreciate where they are coming from. What they fail to realise is that none of us are truly the masters of our own destiny. We all live with two opposing forces at work in our lives. While we may think we are our own boss, listen for just a second to what Jesus declared in John 10:10 "The thief's purpose is to steal and kill and destroy. My purpose is to give them a rich and satisfying life."

I continually see the battle for souls in that one verse. When we open our eyes, we all can agree that this world is both beautiful and evil. Man's inhumanity creates war, starvation, hatred, greed, selfishness and the list could go on and on and on. Jesus said that there is an enemy called Satan who comes to steal, kill and destroy life. When Adam and Eve rebelled against God, it wasn't just a mistake, it wasn't just a bite and it wasn't just a silly thing they did. The enormity of that one moment of rebellion affected the entire creation and made the way for all manner of evil to enter this world.

God warned Adam; "The moment you eat of the fruit of the Tree of Knowledge of Good and Evil you will die." Please note, God did not say "I will kill you." In effect He was saying you will press the self-destruct button and the result of that will be death and every form of evil known will enter into your world. It is incredible that people ask, "If there is a God, why did He allow X or Y to happen?" when God forewarned man of the consequences of his actions.

When I was about 5 or 6 years old I was told not to try and reach the ball that was taken away from me and placed on top of a very large kitchen dresser. I could not quite reach it as I stood on the little shelf between the lower and top part of the dresser so I decided to open the door and stand on the top shelf. As I stretched to reach the ball, suddenly the top half of the dresser began to fall toward me, I fell backward and the dresser fell on me. I remember a mighty crash and as I crawled out from under the dresser my thoughts turned to my parents who I thought would kill me.

I ran to the kitchen and sat on a chair just as my mum and dad came in from the front of the house. "What was that crash?" they said as they went into the dining room. The place was a mess, there was glass everywhere. "What happened, was that you? Did you do this? Were you trying to get that ball?" They did not believe me when I protested that I thought it was the cat that knocked over the dresser and when they noticed blood coming from my foot my game was up. Now can you image their reaction if I began to blame them for my cut toe? It was my fault and my fault alone; even though I was injured, I was guilty.

God said to Adam "You will die!" It was a simple enough statement and it was also true. Adam ignored God's warning and consequently there was a crash. Adam and Eve fell from their place. Suddenly their eyes were opened and they knew they had sinned and rebelled against God. Finally they were removed from God's presence as a barrier of sin had now formed between God and man. The 'god of this world' had certainly deceived Adam and Eve but in the midst of God's anger He declared that a day would come when He would make a way for the relationship to be restored. When a man or women, boy or girl accepts and receives Jesus Christ as their own personal Saviour, a miracle takes place. They are immediately restored into the household of God. They have simply returned to God, through Christ and come under new ownership.

When Paul, an Apostle, wrote to the Christians at Corinth he said this;

"God has paid a high price for you, so don't be enslaved by the world."
1 Corinthians 7:23.

I was once told that the value of anything is determined by the purchase price. Therefore if you bought a car worth about £150, in truth, what kind of car would you expect to receive? What about if the car you bought cost £25,000? I am sure you would place much more value upon it.

Consider this. God has given everything to purchase you back into His Kingdom. So what value has He placed on your soul? He waits to invest His love, mercy and grace in you for the purpose of improving every area of your life. The only real question to be asked is this: do you want to stay under the ownership of Satan whose only objective is to steal, kill and destroy everything good in your life, or do you want to be restored to God? New ownership is available. Only you can make that choice.

Chapter Ten

THE LAST ROUND

"That's it!" I thought to myself as I came off the course. My round once more was a disaster. I couldn't get the ball off the tee; I just knocked it along the ground. I couldn't putt and I just felt as though I was wasting my time trying to continue to play this 'silly' game. Many golfing friends have felt the same at one time or another.

Geordie, Keith, Chris and others for one reason or another have thought about putting the clubs away and giving up. Some have taken a break for a while and come back refreshed. Others however have finally given up for good. John, who was one of our seniors, finally called it a day as he reached his 80th birthday. In his prime he was a good player and even in his late seventies he still had a good eye for the game. The last time I saw John on the course though he looked very tired. He had only played a few holes but he was struggling to get around. His breathing became more difficult on some of the slightly uphill holes and I knew he wasn't enjoying the day, his golf, or the experience. He only managed to play twelve holes and as he walked of the green for the last time he knew that was it.

I certainly miss John around Merlin. In his prime he was an excellent player and without being intrusive he was always willing to give the odd suggestion or two to any player who was looking to improve his game. "I would have loved to have coached you thirty years ago" he said to me when we were once playing a round together, then he added "but it's too late now." I didn't feel inclined to ask if that was a compliment or not as we continued our match.

The 10th at Merlin is an interesting hole; it's a par 4 off the yellow tees and a par 5 off the white tees. As it has a slight dog leg to the left, the temptation shot is to hit the ball as close to the left side as possible. Hit it well on that line, and you can turn it into an easy par 4 for the average golfer. Too far left and you could be out of bounds in the field or in heavy rough near the hedge that runs all the way down the left hand side of the hole. I decided to take the tight line one morning and thankfully I managed to hit a perfect shot. It took off like one of the jets which often flew out of Newquay Airport. If only I could hit the ball like that all of the time!

As I walked toward my ball, I suddenly saw an inscription on a piece of granite rock which I had never noticed previously. In essence it read "In Memory of Wally Gittins who died near this spot 12-03-02." I stopped and read it over again; "Wally Gittins died near this spot...." I had no idea or memory of such an event at Merlin. When I finally finished my round and got back to the clubhouse I asked Bill about Wally.

"Oh Wally, he was a lovely man, a real gentlemen. He didn't hit the ball far, but he was usually straight down the middle" Bill replied. "I noticed an inscription on the 10th" I continued. "Yes, he died. Just keeled over. We tried to help him, but he had gone. The Emergency Services came but it was too late. Shame really, he was a lovely man."

Wally never knew that morning as he hit his ball on the first tee that he was about to play his last round of golf. The fact remains, without sounding too morbid, that a day will come when we will all play our last round of golf, or we will have had our last cup of coffee, or our last meal. We cannot deny the fact it will happen, but what happens next? Some believe the answer is nothing; the end is the end. Once you take your last breath, then that is it. Done. It is finished and your life is over. The majority of people will say honestly, "I don't know, I believe there is something, but I don't know." The Christian will say, "I do know and I have a tremendous future."

At death, we do use some interesting terminology. We say things like, "So-and-so has gone on" or "They have passed on." We will always hear someone say "Well he/she is looking down on us from a better place." So, in the heart of most is found the belief that there is something more when this life is finally over.

The Bible is very clear and precise about the subject and although little is said about what Heaven will look or feel like, much is said however about the need to receive eternal life as a gift from God. Eternal life in Heaven is not the automatic outcome for all people who die and the Bible is very clear on this. I have, throughout this little book, written about the need for personal salvation. I have said much about the fact that we all have sinned and how Jesus came to restore us again to God, once the justice of God was met. I have explained how it is possible to have a brilliant round in life and still be disqualified from Heaven.

When Paul wrote his letters to the various churches, he wrote this to the Christians in Rome. It is interesting to read his words; "The wages of sin is death, but the free gift of God is eternal life through Christ Jesus our Lord." (Rom 6:23) In this one verse Paul the apostle makes it clear for all, "Eternal life is through Christ Jesus our Lord."

The fact is that Jesus, after he had died on the cross, did not remain in the grave. He came to give us eternal life and this was revealed through His own resurrection. If He had not risen again and overcome the final enemy, death itself, then none of us would be able to receive God's gift of eternal life. The religious leaders were terrified of the prophecy of Jesus coming to pass so they went to see Pilate. They told him "Sir, we remember what that deceiver once said while He was still alive. 'After three days I will rise from the dead. So we request that you seal the tomb until the third day. This will prevent His disciples from coming and stealing His body and then telling everyone He was raised from the dead! If that happens, we'll be worse off than we were at first." Pilate replied, "Take guards and secure it the best you can." So they sealed the tomb and posted guards to protect it.

Jesus was laid in a rich man's grave given by Joseph of Arimathea, who was a follower of Jesus. He went to Pilate and asked for His body. His followers had run away from the scene and all except John, had deserted Him. Peter, one of the main spokespersons amongst the disciples, had already denied Him three times, just as Jesus had told him he would. Jesus died a lonely death. He was forsaken. Joseph took the body down from the cross, wrapped it in a long sheet of linen cloth and laid it in his own new tomb that had been carved out of a rock. You can almost feel the heart of this man. He was a follower of Jesus and desired to show one final act of respect by giving Jesus at least a decent burial. Isaiah the prophet had written almost 700 years previously about Jesus: "He had done no wrong and hadn't deceived anyone. He was buried like a criminal; He was put in a rich man's grave." (Isaiah 53:9)

However when Mary Magdalene and the other Mary went out to visit the tomb there was a great earthquake! An angel of the Lord came down from Heaven, rolled aside the stone and sat on it. His face shone like lightening, and His clothing was white as snow. The guards were terrified and so overcome with the power of God that they fell down like dead men. The angel spoke to the women and his words were the most significant words ever spoken on the face of the earth. "Do not be afraid!" he said. "I know you are looking for Jesus, who was crucified. He isn't here! He is risen from the dead just as He said He would."

The final enemy - death itself, has been overcome. For the Christian this is the whole purpose of the gospel or good news of why Jesus came. The final act is complete, the last green is played and all who turn to Christ can be saved. Their names are written in the Book of Life. Heaven is their final destiny and they can not only know the very presence of God today as they turn to him, but they can be assured of an eternal destiny and a wonderful future in Heaven.

It is important at this stage to write that it is not God's intention for anyone to perish, in fact the opposite is true. God loves you and has a great plan and purpose for your life. Even today, God is knocking at the door of your heart. Will you open it and let Him in?

I love playing golf. I have tried to share in this little book some of the great highs and great joys that I have experienced through playing this game. For those of you who play golf, you will know exactly what I mean.

I also love people. I've smiled many times while writing this book as I've recalled these stories and some of the great characters that I've met along the way.

Most of all though, I love God. He's been my inspiration and constant companion for over 40 years. I hope that as you have read this book, you have not felt 'preached at' in any way. That has never been my desire. Rather I have tried my best to explain clearly the most important message you could ever hear.

A day will come when you and I will play our final round on this little planet called earth. I hope, if it is God's will, that we may find a golf course or two in Heaven, and that you will join me there as we may even play 'A Round with God'.

Appendix

Having read this book, you may feel that you would like to receive Jesus as your Lord and Saviour. If so, why don't you take a few moments right now and pray this simple prayer:

> " Lord Jesus,
> I come to you now and confess my need of salvation. I acknowledge that I have sinned and that I need your grace, your love, and your forgiveness. Thank you for dying on the cross for me.
> Come into my life Lord Jesus, and make me a new person.
> From this moment on I put my faith in you and ask you to be the Lord of my life.
> Thank you for saving me.
> Amen."

If you have prayed that prayer I would love to hear from you. I would also love to hear from you if you have further questions about the Christian journey.

You can contact me by email: matt@aroundwithgod.com